New York University
Institute of Comparative Law

PROCEDURE AND DEMOCRACY

STUDIES IN COMPARATIVE LAW

New York University
Institute of Comparative Law

FRENCH ADMINISTRATIVE LAW AND THE COMMON-LAW WORLD
THE CODE NAPOLEON AND THE COMMON-LAW WORLD
PROCEDURE AND DEMOCRACY

*P*rocedure and *D*emocracy

By Piero Calamandrei

Professor of Law, University of Florence

Translated by
John Clarke Adams *and* Helen Adams

Foreword to the American Reader
by Edmond Cahn

NEW YORK UNIVERSITY PRESS
Washington Square
1956

Foreword to the
American Reader

THIS, I think, is the sort of book you have been hoping to find and savor. If you are already acquainted with Piero Calamandrei's personality or his works, you need no introduction; you know already what a rich store of pleasure he can concentrate in a few compact pages. But if you happen to be a stranger to his name and writings, it may be useful for me to hold you a moment and tell you briefly about him.

If Calamandrei were like most other lawyers, I should be happy to emphasize the strictly professional side of his accomplishments. It is true that he is a full professor of civil procedure at the University of Florence, that he is an extraordinarily successful practitioner, that he was a member of the Italian Constitutional Assembly and subsequently a member of the Parliament, that he has been president of the National Council of Lawyers, and—to put it as shortly as possible—enjoys an illustrious international reputation in the law and philosophy of civil procedure. Yet, when I have listed all these achievements, I have been telling you only about Calamandrei the expert, and Calamandrei the man remains to be described.

As you read *Procedure and Democracy*, you will notice not only flashes of humor and charm of style but also deep compassion and penetrating insight. In this book, Calamandrei expresses an intrepid democratic faith and a reasoned, discerning optimism. Nevertheless, as in everything else he has written, he gives us intimations and overtones of the tragic or pathetic side of human experience. While, for instance, he rebukes the kind of presiding judge who drifts into a state of inattention and somnolence, he simultaneously grieves with him over the inroads of advancing age and the tedium inflicted by long-winded lawyers. Sagely Calamandrei understands and compassionates the winners as well as the losers in this, our world.

I wish there were space here to write in detail about Calamandrei's humanism. Meeting him in person is a very impressive experience. How, one mutters, is it that this twentieth-century liberal jurist is able to embody the most cultivated and courtly qualities of the sixteenth-century Renaissance? Here in modern Florence he lives in easy companionship with the heroic minds of ancient Greece and Rome. Wearing his classical culture lightly and unobtrusively, he values the ancients as did our Henry Thoreau, who said "They only talk of forgetting them who never knew them. It will be soon enough to forget them when we have the learning and the genius which will enable us to attend to and appreciate them. . . . The works of the great poets have never yet been read by mankind, for only great poets can read them. They have only been read as the multitude read the stars, at most astrologically, not astronomically. Most men have learned to read to serve a paltry convenience, as they have learned to cipher in order to keep accounts and not be cheated in trade; but of reading as a noble intellectual exercise they know little or nothing; yet this only is reading, in a high sense, not that which lulls us as a luxury and suffers the nobler faculties to sleep the while, but what we have to stand on tiptoe to read and devote our most alert and wakeful hours to." This is authentic humanism.

But I must not give you the impression that Calamandrei has adopted the life of a cloistered scholar. That would be very misleading. On the contrary, he is a practicing lawyer through and through. The hourly and daily experiences of many years have endowed him with wisdom about courts, lawyers, clients, procedure, and justice. He brings his experience to whatever he writes or reads: just as reading can prepare one to do, doing and observing can prepare one to read. Practice is the great academy where—if anywhere—a lawyer may acquire discernment, sharpen insight, sensitize compassion, recognize mischiefs, concoct remedies, and learn to become aware when he approaches the edge of the possible.

To say that Calamandrei is humane and humanistic and lawyerlike does not provide an adequate picture—unless one notes also that he is devotedly *Tuscan.* I suppose every educated American reserves some special place in his affections for Florence and Tuscany, homelands of the mind and spirit. Yet grateful though we are for the cultural inheritance, we can scarcely hope to appreciate Tuscany as Calamandrei does; that would be exacting too much of ourselves. Consequently, I do not attempt to plumb the depth of our author's patriotism. Instead, I shall add an appendix to this introduction. The appendix will appear in Calamandrei's own words, and will consist of the apostrophe to Tuscany with which he concludes his *Inventario della Casa di Campagna.*[1] It tells of his love for the Tuscan landscape and people, and it demonstrates—quite effectively, I think—why there is an old saying that Italian is the language of eloquence.

There are so many varied and penetrating insights in *Procedure and Democracy* that each reader may select his own favorites. For example, some students of comparative law will be attracted to the passages about the reforms and ideals of Cesare Beccaria, because Justice William O. Douglas of our Supreme Court has recently emphasized Beccaria's influence on Thomas Jefferson.[2] Other readers will discover, perhaps with astonishment, that the much-vaunted Continental system of "career judges" discloses

[1] Florence: Le Monnier (1941).
[2] *Ullmann v. United States,* 350 U.S. 422 (1956).

serious drawbacks in practical application. On one page or another, there are perceptions enough to satisfy a multitude of interests. By way of example, let me mention only two of Calamandrei's many sagacious points.

In Chapter V, with the boldness of a prophet, he compels us to face and recognize the single greatest obstacle standing in the path of procedural reform. What he has to say is brilliant, incontrovertibly true—and most disconcerting. The obstacle consists in the unpleasant fact that, *by and large,* lawyers do not trust one another, judges do not trust lawyers, and lawyers do not trust judges. Of course, there are a certain number of commendable exceptions; but law reform cannot thrive on exceptions. Calamandrei's generalization is completely valid, and as long as it remains valid, reform of procedure will be slow, sporadic, and insecure. Calamandrei's discussion of this problem presents a challenge to every judge and lawyer in the United States.

In another very impressive passage, Calamandrei denounces "that frightful counterfeit of justice which in modern terminology could be called the 'totalitarian' process." Of the totalitarian process he says: "Here the parties are merely figurative elements that serve to increase the spectacular aspects of the rite, and the will of the judge is everything; and his decision, instead of being the final product of the judicial process, evolving from the contrast of opposing wills, and therefore uncertain and undetermined while the trial is in progress, is the arbitrary act of a single will, which stages the trial in order to give an illusory retrospective justification for a decision that has already been reached." Americans know that totalitarian process is not necessarily confined to totalitarian countries. . . .

I believe anyone who reads this book will share my sense of gratitude to Dr. John Clarke Adams. A few years ago, Dr. Adams, together with Mr. C. Abbott Phillips, Jr., prepared a splendidly readable translation of Calamandrei's *Elogio dei Giudici* (*Eulogy of Judges*). Consequently, when New York University School of Law projected an English version of *Processo e Democrazia* (*Procedure and Democracy*), we appealed to Dr. Adams to serve again as translator. Fortunately, he consented. With the collaboration of his wife, Mrs. Helen Adams, he has produced the present skillful and attractive text. Yes, we know the old Italian maxim which says: *traduttore, traditore* ("translator, traitor"). Yet see how Dr. Adams has refuted it! He has shown that, far from being a predestined "traitor," a sensitive translator may assume the role of illuminator, decorator, disseminator, authentic interpreter, and faithful spokesman.

This book is published in English under the auspices of the Institute of Comparative Law of New York University School of Law. My brilliant colleague, Professor Bernard Schwartz, Director of the Institute, has fostered the undertaking from its inception. Professors Calamandrei and Schwartz join me here in sending fraternal greetings to the law faculty of the National University of Mexico, where these chapters were delivered as lectures in February 1952.

In *Procedure and Democracy* the United States receives a superb specimen of Europe's mature juristic thought. Facing as we must the dark corners of a confused and insecure epoch, we need to borrow all the light that other legal systems can lend. We need to follow the counsel of John Milton, who said, "As wine and oil are imported to us from abroad, so must ripe understanding, and many civil virtues, be imported into our minds from foreign writings, and examples of best ages: we shall else miscarry still, and come short in the attempts of any great enterprise."

New York University   Edmond Cahn

Calamandrei's apostrophe to his native Tuscany

Paese discreto e pensieroso, dove ogni colle, quantunque svariato alla vista da pinete o da vigne, chiude nel suo segreto una stanza sepolcrale scavata nel tufo, dentro alla quale, sdraiati sullo stesso letto di pietra, marito e moglie, colla testa compostamente appoggiata sulla mano, si scambiano in eterno un ambiguo sorriso di statue che non vuol parere dolore, poichè anche la morte è da millennî composta e pudica in questo paese, dove sono uguali, a chi li guarda in lontananza sui poggi, i viali di cipressi che portano alle ville e quelli che portano ai camposanti; e dove le vecchie case conservano ancora la porta del morto, dalla quale chi se va può uscir per suo conto, senza disturbare chi resta. Paese dove ogni sorriso sfuma in mestizia, ed ogni lacrima, per non dar noia a chi può vedere, cerca di nascondersi in celia; dove le pene e le gioie più disparate, le vicende più grandi e le più umili, lontane di secoli o nate con noi, si ritrovano livellate e ricomposte in un'armonia casalinga che abolisce le distanze e i tempi e fa sentire che nulla importa o tutto importa nello stesso modo: i nostri morti e i nostri figliuoli, gli incontri della nostra infanzia e gli addii della nostra vecchiaia, i canti delle veglie sulle aie notturne, gli ipogei nascosti e i fiori che si abbelliscono delle loro ceneri, i nostri lutti, il nostro amore, il passato e l'avvenire, le nostre speranze, la nostra libertà: Toscana, dolce patria nostra.

Contents

1. The rational basis of the rules of legal procedure. 2. The requirement that each legal process reach a decision, even when this cannot be achieved by common sense. 3. "The rationalization of power" in the judicial process. 4. The importance of custom in constitutional practice. 5. The importance of custom in judicial practice. 6. The general theory of procedure. 7. The judicial process and justice.

1. The dramatic aspects of the judicial process. 2. Impartiality, the essential characteristic of the judge. 3. Various methods for assuring impartiality. 4. The law of the individual case. 5. Justice and politics. 6. Justice *secundum leges*. 7. The judicial syllogism. 8. Unpredictability of the judgment. 9. Insufficiency of the purely logical conception of the judgment, even under the rule of law. 10. The decision viewed as a product of the judge's conscience.

PROCEDURE AND DEMOCRACY

1. Legal Procedure and Judicial Custom

O NCE during a discussion with my students I had occasion to remark that legal procedure, both civil and criminal, is nothing but an authoritatively imposed *method* (and the science of legal procedure a *methodology*) for attaining justice—a method of reasoning established by the law that the parties and judges must follow step by step according to a certain prescribed and logically coordinated order, for the purpose of reaching a just decision; and the legal process is only an "operation" carried out according to this method.

On close examination the rules of legal procedure are seen to be essentially nothing but maxims of logic and common sense, findings of a technical nature that have been made into binding rules. After all (I said jokingly to my students), from the standpoint of logic there is little difference between the codes of civil and criminal procedure that teach us how to "proceed" in order to obtain justice, and certain elementary technical manuals that teach the "procedure" (note that even the word is the same) to be followed in some art or craft, entitled, for example, "How to Grow Roses" or "How to Become a Photographer" or "How to Become an Underwater Fisherman."

At this point a student asked a question that might have seemed naive but that was actually both pertinent and perspicacious. If the law of legal procedure can be reduced to maxims of logic and common sense, he asked, why is it necessary to work so hard to master it and to translate into binding rules and complicated theories those principles of reason that are part of the natural heritage of all men?

Every hour of the day men are faced with practical problems that can be decided only by the use of reason; at every step in life there arises a doubt, and with this doubt an occasion to use one's logical faculties. Why in all these instances are men free to reason as best they can without the state's attempting to oblige them to follow a prescribed method?

When we determine the authenticity of a disputed painting, when we diagnose a serious illness, when we found a great industrial concern, or when we put a new invention into operation, there arise problems and moments of doubt that can be resolved only by investigation and by reason. In these instances men sit around a table and use their reason and common sense to reach the truth; opposing views meet head on; hypotheses are refuted; but in the end, as a result of free discussion, the truth is found, doubts are overcome, and the problem is solved. Why does the state not feel the need to intervene in these instances to fix the order of the discussion and of the speakers? It is not that the problems are less important, for the decisions reached may involve a man's life or even the political fate of a people.

How does one answer this question? It is true that the law of legal procedure is essentially a technique of good reasoning before the court; but if in this instance the technique is regulated by the state and imposed on the public (the technical rules thus being transformed into legal norms), it is so because the end sought by this technical procedure is the realization of justice, the highest and most solemn office of the state, the office through which the state assures peace in the society: the *fundamentum rei publicae.*

The judgment of the court is also a work of human reason, and judicial logic is no different from that which men use to resolve the other problems that face them in their everyday life. But although the judicial decision springs from man's reason, it is a monopoly and a responsibility that the state assumes. Justice then is also a product of reason; but it is an official reason, regulated by the state.

Therefore the state has been unwilling to permit the ways of rendering justice, which involve the authority and prestige of the state, to be left to improvisation and to the vagaries of individual preference; it has felt obliged to prescribe the techniques of legal procedure in a system of binding rules, of which the *corpus* is the law of legal procedure; and in transforming these techniques into uniform legal norms it has wished to make sure that the method by which the most august of its missions, that of rendering justice, is fulfilled is always consonant with reason—a reason of state, reduced to binding procedures, and the same for all.

If the law must be the same for all in the sense that the general and abstract rule should be applied equally to all similar concrete circumstances, it is not conceivable that the technical procedure which serves for the application of the law to these concrete cases should operate differently according to the varying perceptions of the parties to the dispute, nor that the equilibrium of the pleading should be disturbed either by the overbearing actions of the stronger party or by the subterfuge of the more devious. The law of legal procedure had its origin when the state first felt obliged to intervene as an umpire in the trial by combat, to ensure a fair battle, and later, when combat by arms was transformed into verbal contest, it continued to intervene in order to ensure a fair trial.

But it should also be borne in mind that judicial reasoning differs from other types of reasoning in that in all instances a decision is required. After a long discussion at the bedside of the patient, physicians may conclude with the honest admission that a sure diagnosis is not possible; but the judge cannot terminate the trial with a *non liquet.* Where the methods of common logic do not succeed in solving the problem, where they must retreat before the insuperable obstacle of a doubt stronger than any reasoning, the judicial process establishes a sure method for arriving at a decision. In order to fix jural relations with certitude— and to succeed in this is an essential condition of social peace —the state normally makes use of the rules of natural logic as codified in the laws of legal procedure; but because of the importance of the end product, social peace, where natural logic is insufficient the state is disposed to discard it and to adopt other procedures for arriving at a decision; and so by means of ingenious procedural mechanisms, it creates a kind of "artificial" or "official" logic that serves to resolve all questions at issue, even those that common reason would call insoluble.

This concept, according to which legal procedure is considered a codified form of logic, brings to mind a phenomenon that attracted the attention of constitutional lawyers in the years immediately following the First World War. Mirkine Guetzévitch, one of the first to grasp its significance, referred to it as *la tendance à la rationalisation du pouvoir.*[1] In the democratic constitutions of continental Europe written in the aftermath of World War I there is a tendency to express in written norms those principles and techniques of proper procedure that in the British system, the model for all these constitutions, are part of the unwritten law, sanctioned by custom and by the integrity and civic education of the governing class.

This tendency *à la rationalisation du pouvoir,* which the consti-

---

[1] Boris Mirkine Guetzévitch, *Les nouvelles tendances du droit constitutionnel* (2d ed.; Paris: Librairie Générale de Droit, 1936), ch. 1; and "Essai synthétique," in Boris Mirkine Guetzévitch, *Les constitutions européennes* (Paris: Presses Universitaires de France, 1951), Vol. I, pp. 3-154, at 14.

tutional lawyers have studied as a recent phenomenon in the fields of legislative and executive power, is an old friend in the judicial field. For many centuries, perhaps for thousands of years, customary techniques have been gradually codified in law, and the remarkable increase in studies of legal procedure in the last century is the best witness to this gradual change of emphasis from "procedure" in the sense of the technique of practicing attorneys, to the "systematization" of the judicial process, understood as a science of rational principles.

The whole history of the legal process, from the *formulae* of Roman law to the *positiones* of common law, from the Italian *statuti* to the French *coutumes*, up to the preparation of the codes, is in substance the history of the transformation of judicial practice into the law of legal procedure; from the *practica fori*, from the *stylus curiae*, has gradually emerged an architectonic system of formal rules that, although they may have lost all apparent connection with the functions they once fulfilled, are still the translation into juridical formulae of practices based on common sense. It is enough to recall how the system of legal proof, with its complex and detailed rules for evaluating evidence, was derived from the intermediate law of the period between the Justinian Code and the modern code, in order to understand how at that time a gradual progress from what one might call pragmatism to judicial rationalism was already under way in the judicial process.

The reason that this tendency toward the "rationalization" of power was apparent in the judicial process earlier than in the other functions of the state is easily explained. It has often been pointed out that if human justice is to perform its clarifying and pacifying mission in society, it must not only be just but must *appear* to be so; that if persons on trial are to submit without rebellion to the terrible omnipotence of justice, they must believe that the judge is an almost divine being, different from other men, endowed with supernatural virtues before which human reason must give way. This is the explanation of the almost religious mystery that in primitive times surrounded the pronouncements of the judges, who sat on high on their thrones and whose voices descended from afar (like the voice of the invisible Sibyl, echoing through the vaults of the cavern); it is the explanation of the spectacular and almost liturgic character of judicial rites, traces of which are still apparent today in the pomp and circumstance of the court, in the wig and the gown, or in the theatrical or almost ecclesiastical architecture of certain courtrooms.

But when the judge descends from heaven to earth and we see that he, too, is a man, then, in order to give value to his judgment, we begin to seek in the ever more precise mechanisms of the judicial process the safeguards to assure that each decision will always be the product of reason, rather than an arbitrary action.

In early Italian the word "reason" was synonymous with justice; to "render reason" meant to do justice, and in some northern Italian cities the building where justice is meted out is still called the *Palazzo della ragione* (Palace of Reason).

The same constitutional lawyers who after the First World War began to show an interest in the problem of the rationalization of power are beginning today, however, to question its usefulness. After seeing the manner in which the constitutions established after the First World War have functioned, and after watching the early attempts to put the constitutions resulting from the Second World War into effect, the most authoritative exponents of this school now seem to recognize that the belief that the political life of a country can be imprisoned within the rigid bounds of rational norms inscribed in the constitution is a utopian illusion. In the most recent European constitutions attempts have been made to reduce to written norms English parliamentary practice, that "religion without dogma," unique both for its irrational and pragmatic character and for its elasticity, and incapable of being contained within any rigorous systematization. But the political experience of the last decade has already shown that apparently identical constitutional formulae applied by different peoples give essentially different results. When the English parliamentary system is inserted in the constitutions of continental Europe it is like a tree transplanted to another climate; it is no longer recognizable. Experience has shown conclusively that in spite of the schematic rigidity of rationalized constitutions, the political life of each nation continues to operate according to its own irrational proclivities, pre-established constitutional procedures notwithstanding.

Although not so long ago one was hardly permitted to grant custom even the power to integrate written law, in the last few decades legal theorists, especially in France, have returned to the idea that among the sources of constitutional law custom should be given first place, and are again saying *"sur le terrain du mécanisme politique, la coutume est presque tout."*[2]

The Italian experience of the last few years has shown the correctness of this point of view. The political reality of modern Italy is not a true reflection of Italy's written constitution. Five years after the promulgation of the constitution many of the institutions it minutely regulates, such as the Constitutional Court[3] and the regional governments, are still in the platonic state of unrealized desires. Constitutional formulae are living forces only when the political power that gives them life is flowing through them. Without this lifeblood they become atrophied and die.[4]

[2] "In the field of political relations, custom is almost everything." These words, written by Saleilles in 1903, are cited by Marcel Prélot in the preface of the first volume of Mirkine Guetzévitch, *Les constitutions européennes.*

[3] Translator's note: The Constitutional Court was finally established in 1956. Professor Calamandrei was counsel for one of the petitioners in the first case to be heard by the court. In this case police regulations limiting freedom of the press were declared unconstitutional.

[4] See Piero Calamandrei, "Insensibilità costituzionale," *Il ponte,* VIII (1952).

A similar phenomenon occurs in the judicial process. Ostensibly the whole of legal procedure is found in the codes; and on the basis of codified law, doctrine builds monumental constructions as majestic as Gothic cathedrals. But these constructions are not the real judicial process. *The judicial process is more than that.*

When law school graduates begin their apprenticeship in a lawyer's office immediately after receiving their university degrees, they find that the judicial process is actually quite different from what they learned in school. When they enter the courtroom for the first time they are not able to recognize in the apparently inconsequent actions they see going on about them the symmetry they found in the learned words of their professors.

I still remember the admonishment I was given by my father's old clerk when I was beginning my apprenticeship just after finishing law school. This man could hardly read and write, but after spending fifty years in the anterooms of justice he had become expert in the practices of the trade.

Coming into my room and finding me immersed in a pile of books, he shook his head slowly and said to me with a sigh, "Poor Signor Dottore! Don't waste your time reading books. If you ask me, it's experience that counts."

"It's experience that counts." At that time I rejected with youthful scorn the unsolicited advice of that old man. But now, forty years later, I realize that those simple words contain a great truth. Today I must recognize the fact that the judicial process as it is written in the Code is only an empty mold, which produces different results according to the particular substance poured into it. Thus the most varied procedures can come out of the same mold in the different judicial districts of the same state, and although each pretends to be the faithful realization of the same law of procedure, the difference among them is greater than that of children of the same mother.

In Italy, even after the adoption of the new Code of Civil Procedure (1942), the actual practice in different parts of the country varies, at times to a notable degree. The Milanese courts continue to follow their traditional procedure, which is jokingly called "the Ambrosian rite," from the name of St. Ambrose, patron saint of the city, and in Naples the legal process, successfully resisting all attempts at change, preserves a clearly recognizable local physiognomy based on its traditional practices, that might be called "the rite of San Gennaro," the patron saint of Naples. The influence of local traditions on legal practice is responsible for the divergent applications of the written rules of procedure, increasing the importance of some, lessening that of others, and even disregarding some entirely.

There are, for example, two provisions in our Code of such great theoretical interest that every law professor is sure to expatiate on them. One is Article 113, which empowers the judge, on the request of both parties, to decide a case according to equity rather than according to law. The other is Article 360, which makes it possible, on the request of both parties, to send a case on appeal directly from the trial court, *omisso medio,* to the Court of Cassation. Parliament believed that these two innovations, which give the parties the power to streamline the legal process, would meet with the favor of counsel; but this was an illusion. These innovations are unknown to legal practice; in the ten years that the new Code has been in effect I do not believe that the parties (or their counsel) have even once agreed to ask the judge to decide according to equity or to take an appeal directly to the Court of Cassation *per saltum,* thus avoiding the step of an intermediate appellate judgment.

In this way procedures duly written in the law may become atrophied and disappear in practice, while, conversely, methods of procedure can spring up in practice that are unknown to the written law. In southern Italy, from Rome down, in both the lower and higher courts the discussion of a case frequently takes place *"in camera di consiglio,"* that is, in the judge's chambers, while in the courts of northern Italy the discussion, when it is held at all, always takes place openly in the courtroom, as the Code prescribes (Article 275).

Sometimes practice can do even more. It can gradually alter the entire purpose of a reform and paralyze all attempts at innovation with a passive resistance more lethal than open rebellion. Past experience shows that practice has a delaying rather than an accelerating influence and that it resists the reforms by which parliament hopes to speed up the legal process. Each time a law has attempted to provide a special summary proceeding for the most urgent cases because of the length of time consumed in the regular proceedings, this summary proceeding has gradually replaced the regular procedure in practice; but at the same time it has taken over from the old procedure all its possibilities for delay, disregarding its summary character, which, as its name implies, was intended by parliament to be its basic virtue. Practice tends to complicate the judicial process as well as to slow it down. Although, in the interest of simplicity and speed, the law has provided for oral proceedings *inter praesentes,* the bureaucratic practice of exchanging briefs *inter absentes* has actually been reintroduced. According to the present Italian Code the investigatory phase of the civil process should always be oral (Art. 180), but because of the prejudice against oral proceedings shared by lawyers and judges the old written procedures are returning to use and this phase is again assuming the form of a series of exchanges of briefs. Other discrepancies between the written law and current practice can be found in criminal procedure, and these are even more seriously at variance with the principles established in the written law. To give a single example, the investigation of crimes and the indictment of criminals, which according to the Code of Criminal Procedure should be under the control of the judges, has actually been turned over to the police in the last few decades, both in Italy and in France, in spite of the written law. In this manner the clock has been turned back several centuries and criminal procedure has again become an inquisitorial procedure before the police.

The degree to which the customs of the people can be reflected in the judicial process did not escape the penetrating mind of Giuseppe Chiovenda, who in his *Principii* pointed out:[5]

"the civil process is the most delicate of all legal institutions; as a means of distributing the goods of this life through the application of the law, it occupies a central position between private law and public law; and since it is so complex an institution that it includes a political and a social side as well as a legal one, the slightest changes in the moral, political or social environment are reflected in its operation. For example, to the degree that honesty and good faith are dominant in social relations, that there is mutual trust between citizens and the government, and that people are inclined to look into the heart of a matter, disregarding superficial formalities—to that degree trials can proceed speedily and will depend less on formal safeguards. Therefore, because forms created for a given moment of history are not adapted to other periods, and the legal profession is eminently conservative with respect to procedural formalities, it is easier in this than in any other field for disharmony to exist between a rule of law and practical requirements. There are rules of procedure that no longer have any reason to exist. This does not justify the interpreter in refusing to apply them, but he should bring them to the attention of parliament for the necessary reforms. There are other rules of procedure that, although still useful, have a different function from their orig-

[5] Giuseppe Chiovenda, *Principii di diritto processuale civile* (3d ed.; Napoli: Iovene), p. 131.

inal one, not in their content (that would be equivalent to modifying them) but in their purposes; and this can affect the limits and the manner of their application, and teach us to use the ancient doctrine with care."

Custom is considered here as one of the variable elements that must be taken into account in giving a historical interpretation of the law of procedure as a factor in the evolution of the judicial process. But the practical importance of legal customs may be greater than that claimed for them even by those most aware of their influence. Actually the judicial process is given its typical physiognomy not by the law of procedure but by the habit of mind of those who apply it. The written law is little more than a frame; the relief, with its color and its chiaroscuro, is composed of customs and usages. The words with which Saleilles described constitutional law apply equally to the law of procedure: "... *les textes écrits ne sont guère que la trame très légère sur laquelle travaille et fonctionne la force organisatrice et régulatrice qui met en oeuvre la vie collective d'un pays.*"[6]

"*La vie collective d'un pays*": Even legal procedure is but an aspect of this life, and the law of procedure is but a fragile net whose contours are often distorted by the social realities it contains and attempts to control.

This pressure of social reality that is constantly making itself felt within the formalities of judicial procedure is similarly manifest in any prearranged system for the operation of a government function. Whenever, in securing a declaration of will on the part of the state (be it expressed in a law, a decree, or a judgment), the form and chronology of the various actions to be performed by the persons working to obtain this declaration are pre-established by structural norms, the dialectic succession of these oper-

[6] Raymond Saleilles, "Y a-t-il vraiment une crise de la science politique?" *Revue politique et parlementaire*, XXXVI (1903), 118–119.

ations, regulated by law for the furtherance of that purpose, constitutes a process. Thus we speak of the administrative process to indicate the series of activities that culminate in an administrative act, and we speak of the legislative process to indicate the series of discussions and deliberations which in the end produces a law.[7]

The whole parliamentary system is essentially a "process," a series of "operations" directed toward a certain end. The surprising similarities between judicial procedure and parliamentary procedure are apparent only to those who have had practical experience in the ways of parliament and who discover how much the tactics of political debates resemble pleadings before the court and how many parliamentary battles can be reduced to points of order, *litis ingressum impedientes*. We shall return to this point frequently in the course of this volume. I am certain that the science of legal procedure could benefit greatly from a careful study of its similarities to parliamentary procedure.

There is also a close kinship between parliamentary debates and judicial hearings. True, in the first the emphasis is on speaking and in the second on listening, but essentially the purpose in both instances is that the speaker be heard and the hearer be informed. In hearings, if we are to honor the etymology of the word, the lawyers speak so that the judges may hear; in parliament there must be a government to listen to the deputies, else they would speak to no purpose. (This resemblance in theory carries over into practice as well. Thus it may happen that no one speaks in a hearing, or that no one listens in parliament.)

Every process has this characteristic: that no matter how detailed the rules that regulate its operation, the actions of which

[7] See Costantino Mortati, *Istituzioni di diritto pubblico* (Padova: CEDAM, 1952), ch. v, sec. 3, pp. 26ff., on the legislative process; and Guido Zanobini, *Corso di diritto amministrativo* (6th ed.; Milano: A. Giuffrè, 1952), pp. 218ff., on the administrative process.

it is composed can never be foreseen so exactly that no room is left for individual initiative and discretion. Regardless of how detailed the regulations may be and how faithfully the actions taken follow the prescribed rules, the process is never more than an outline of which the conceptual continuity may be broken up into a series of juxtaposed but discontinuous actions, separated by intervals of time and space; nor is a rigid sequence of actions necessarily prescribed, since frequently the outline itself provides the participants with a choice of alternative actions at a given phase of the process. Furthermore, the succeeding actions are determined by the choice of the previous action, which may be said to condition them.

It is through these minute interstices that custom succeeds in insinuating itself into the legal process, accelerating or retarding its pace. By availing itself of these opportunities for discretion, practice succeeds in transforming or deforming the process even to the extent that it becomes quite the opposite of what the law intended. These are the open windows of the Palace of Reason, through which, despite the best-laid plans, the wind of irrationality blows.

The rules of parliamentary behavior, based on British practice, have been carefully copied in the latest European constitutions. But if we compare the actual procedure during a session of the House of Commons with that of the French or Italian parliament, we immediately become aware that a basically different atmosphere prevails, which is not so much the result of different laws as of different customs and political education.

The same comparison can be made with respect to the legal process. In Italy a trial resembles a theatrical performance; in England it is more like a religious service. During my recent visit to Cambridge University, I was surprised to learn that English universities do not teach legal procedure. Proper court behavior

is not a subject for study; it is learned in practice. It is considered a question of etiquette rather than of knowledge.

After making these comparisons there arises again that sense of discontent, and almost of distress, shared by all the jurists who attended the last International Congress of Civil Procedure in Florence. At the conclusion of our discussions our first impulse was to congratulate ourselves on the promising revival of our studies and on the high level of our research both in Europe and in America, but later we began to wonder: Do these theoretical constructions of ours really aid justice? Are the decisions of the courts more just as a result of these highly refined concepts? Is the judicial process really that precision instrument fabricated from elegant logical abstractions on which we expatiate in our treatises?

Before the closing of that congress—which is memorable also for this reason—we pledged ourselves to work with renewed fervor and to direct our energies not to the perfection of the aesthetics of systematic abstract constructions, but to the realization of justice and the service of the men who thirst for justice.[8]

Now, to maintain this pledge we must become ever more thoroughly persuaded that the object of our studies, the judicial process, is not what parliament imagined it to be in the abstract, but what the men, the judges and the judged, who actually take part in the process, make of it, how they perform it, in the theatrical sense of the word. These persons are not abstractions; they are not identical mechanized puppets—they are live men, each living in his own individual and social world, with his feelings, interests, opinions, and habits—including, unfortunately, even his bad habits.

Even bad habits—this is another point of similarity between

---

[8] See Piero Calamandrei, "Processo e giustizia," in *Atti del Congresso Internazionale di diritto procesuale civile* (Padora: CEDAM, 1953), pp. 9ff.

judicial procedure and parliamentary procedure. Judicial chicanery, which is the degeneration of the judicial process, and "parliamentarianism," which is the degeneration of parliament, are symptoms of the same disease, caused by a deficiency of civic education and social solidarity. When these qualities are lacking, the decay of democratic institutions is inevitable. The danger that threatens democracy is the adoration of abstract reason that was typical of the Enlightenment, which held that reason was sufficient in itself to control the destiny of man.

The truth is—and herein lies the key to the salvation of democratic governments—that propositions of abstract reason, set down in the articles of a democratic constitution, cannot of themselves give life to a democracy; there must also be at work a vigilant and active democratic practice consciously and steadily making of these constitutional principles a reasoned, reasonable, and living reality.

"La démocratie est un comportement, un engagement. Faute de cet engagement, la technique constitutionnelle est morte."[9]

And this is equally true of the code of legal procedure.

[9] "Democracy is a mode of behavior, a commitment. Without this commitment, constitutional method is impotent."—Mirkine Guetzévitch, *Les constitutions européenes,* Vol. I, p. 153.

II. *Justice and Politics:*
Judgments and Sentiment

A T THE END of the preceding chapter I pointed out that for
the proper functioning of the judicial process the practice
of those who are called upon to put the system into effect
is much more important than the technical perfection of the abstract rules that regulate it. Incidentally, a similar statement could
be made with respect to all public institutions, particularly to
those operating in a democracy.

It is commonly said that both the civil and the criminal process
resemble a play in that they are a presentation in dialogue of a
series of incidents performed by different people and divided into
linked episodes, which are brought to final resolution by the
decision, which serves as an epilogue. Actually, its form is not
the only dramatic aspect of the judicial process. Its content is
often a human drama that is, according to the circumstances,
of comic or tragic significance. This explains the morbid interest
of the general public in certain criminal cases and the frequency
with which trial scenes are portrayed on stage and screen.

Now we all know that it is one thing to read the text of a play
and another to see it performed by a great actor who re-creates
and transfigures it. A similar metamorphosis occurs in the judicial
process. The laws of procedure are re-created and transfigured
by the great protagonists of the forensic stage. One difference
remains, however; in the theater every line of the dialogue is
written ahead of time, but in the courtroom the laws of procedure

set down only a number of plots in outline form, one of which must be chosen and filled in by the participants. In this sense the forensic drama is similar to the *commedia dell'arte,* where the actors improvise within the pattern of a pre-established plot.

The most important character in the forensic drama, the true protagonist, is the judge. Silent, impenetrable, and omnipresent, he observes the whole unfolding of the plot, even if he only listens in silence to the discourses of the other actors. But the final word is always his. Everything that has occurred in the trial is summed up and resolved by his decision, which is the epilogue of the drama, or the conclusion of the ceremony. *"Ite, missa est"*: *"ite, iudicatum est."* The judge acts as the *deus ex machina,* as Athena does when she appears in the catharsis of the *Oresteia.*[1]

Let us now examine the function of the judge, both in theory and in practice, in the juridical system of a modern democracy.

From his first appearance at the dawn of civilization the quality that has always seemed inseparable from the very idea of a judge is impartiality.[2] The judge is an independent third party to the dispute, sharing neither the interests nor the passions of the litigants, who examines their dispute objectively, with serenity and detachment. He is an outsider *inter partes,* or better, *supra partes.* He is not motivated by any selfish personal interest related to one of the interests in conflict; rather, he serves the superior interest of the collectivity in the legal and peaceable resolution of the dispute, *ne cives ad arma veniant.* And for this reason it is essential that he be extraneous to the dispute and uninfluenced by the pressures of the parties: *nemo iudex in re propria.*

Although the idea of impartiality is inseparable from the idea of a judge, the theory that a judge must decide *secundum leges* is

[1] See Enrico Redenti, *Intorno al concetto di giurisdizione,* Parma, 1914, pp. 11, 12.
[2] Niceto Alcalá Zamora, *Proceso, autocomposición y autodefesa,* Mexico, 1947, particularly sections 38ff.

not universally held. Judgment *secundum leges* is the most nearly perfected and rationalized method of rendering justice, but it is not the only method, and in the history of judicial institutions judges have used various other criteria or fictions to assure their impartiality, or at least the appearance of it.

In early times the judge was also a priest or soothsayer, who sought aid and inspiration from superstition and magic; he found the motivation of his judgment in the flight of birds or in the palpitating entrails of the sacrifice. The judgment of God, trial by fire, the ordeals, were all expedients for guaranteeing the impartiality of the judgment by the introduction of forces above and beyond human control and earthly concern, such as blind fate or the indifference of the gods. Rabelais' famous judge, Bridoye, who weighed the documents presented by the two litigants and decided in favor of him whose documents were the heavier, achieved a certain impartiality by this method; and the same can be said for the justice of the Turkish *qadi,* who, according to Francesco Guicciardini, judged with closed eyes. Nevertheless, after studying their decisions, the Florentine historian came to the conclusion that their probability of error was no greater than that of the Tuscan judges of his day. "If we suppose that the Turkish judges decide their cases blindly, it follows that in the long run half of them must be just; and this leads to a smaller percentage of unjust decisions than occur in our country, through either the ignorance or the malice of our judges."[3]

Much the same can be said for that time-saving procedure that an ethnologist reports having witnessed while visiting a savage tribe dwelling on the banks of an African lake. When a dispute arose the two litigants were tied to stakes set up on the shore at an equal distance from the water, and left there to await judg-

[3] Francesco Guicciardini, *Ricordi,* Serie seconda, No. 209 (in *Scritti politici e ricordi,* Bari, Laterza, 1933, p. 333).

ment. Before long the judge, an elderly alligator experienced in this work, appeared from out of the water and after looking over the situation slowly crawled toward one of the stakes. The litigant who was eaten had lost his case (with costs).

It is not necessary, however, to resort to these curious, exotic, and possibly fictitious examples to make this point; the judicial systems of the present day offer numerous examples of procedures in which the judge renders justice by methods far removed from the rigorous application of pre-established laws.

In the judicial procedure of continental Europe there are many examples of equity jurisdiction and of arbitration boards,[4] which try to resolve the dispute at hand according to the principles of justice without attempting to find a basis for their decision in the law; for they are not bound by the law, but only by an innate sense of justice that suggests to them the most fitting and equitable solution of the case before them.

This occurs in Italy, for example, when the organs of administrative justice, to which citizens may have recourse against the definitive acts of the public administration, serve in their capacity as judges of the merits of the act. In such instances they are not asked to ascertain its legality but to assess the much less tangible problem of its advisability in the public interest.

In this series of examples of extra-legal justice we should also mention the disciplinary jurisdiction that certain professional associations exercise over their members. The bar associations, for instance, do not judge the professional conduct of lawyers according to legal norms but according to the traditional rules of professional ethics that are only an expression of the common conscience of the bar.

[4] Piero Calamandrei, "Il significato costituzionale delle giurisdizioni di equità," in *Studi sul processo civile* (Padova: CEDAM, 1930), Vol. II, pp. 1ff.

In all these cases the judge finds no ready-made answer in the code; he must seek the solution for the case at hand in his innate sense of justice. The decision is not prefabricated; it must be made to order.

The most obvious example of this phenomenon also comes from contemporary experience, from the conditions under which justice operates in revolutionary periods or in their aftermath.

Take, for instance, Russia after the revolution of 1917. The courts of the Tsarist regime were abolished, the judges and lawyers sent off to shovel snow, and all the codes repealed. The people's courts, composed of workers and peasants, and competent to decide all civil and criminal cases, were created *ex novo,* and were placed in this legal vacuum. Since there were no longer written laws, what was their criterion for judgment? They claimed it was the proletarian conscience, which meant that they judged according to a political criterion, according to the requirements of the political struggle then in progress, and thus even the decisions of the courts became instruments of revolutionary action.

In periods of rapid social change the judge performs a clearly political function. For each case that comes before him he chooses the solution that appears to him the most valuable for the cause of the revolution; he seeks inspiration from his partisan sentiments or resentments. Even today in Soviet Russia, after the reestablishment of a juridical order based on written laws that the judges apply, the political character of the judicial function continues to be emphatically affirmed. The distinction between justice and politics does not exist in Russia in the sense in which it is understood in the liberal tradition of western Europe. Vyshinski, who before becoming a diplomat wrote the official commentaries on the Soviet constitutional system, states openly that the judicial process is one of the instruments of political struggle, first for the success, then for the defense, of the socialist revolution.[5]

A similar phenomenon, particularly affecting criminal procedure, occurred in Nazi Germany when a provision was introduced into the criminal code permitting the judge to convict persons not only for actions classified by law as crimes, but also for actions that the law does not condemn but that the judge holds to be "contrary to the healthy sentiments of the German people."[6]

It is clear that in none of these instances does the judge base his decision on pre-established rules; rather, his decision springs from his feelings as a political being living in society and sharing its economic and moral aspirations, its appetites and antipathies, and its myths, all of which combined can be called the political atmosphere of the period. The transformation of politics into law thus occurs gradually; it is not the work of a forehanded legislator but of a judge who prepares a *lex specialis* for the case at hand. This is what theorists call judge-made law, in which the "sentence," instead of being a product of knowledge and intellect, a cognizance of something already existing, remains true to its etymology and is derived from "sentiment." It is an expression of will based on social experience, in the light of which the judge is led to seek the attainment of a certain social utility through his decision. Even if in deciding the case before him the judge is guided by certain general premises on which he feels his society is agreed, he finds these premises within himself, engraved on his conscience.

This is the law of the individual case. If the judge is a faithful interpreter of his society, this law has the advantage of being

[5] Andrei Ianuarevich Vyshinski, *The Law of the Soviet State* (New York: Macmillan, 1951), especially pp. 497ff.
[6] Section 2 of the criminal code was modified in this sense by the law of June 28, 1935, which became effective September 1, 1935.

perfectly adapted to the special circumstances of the case. Nevertheless it is a gambler's justice, lacking even an approximate predictability, and offering no assurance that similar cases will be given the same treatment. Since each case is treated as if it were unique, the extent of one's rights and obligations, the dividing line between the licit and the illicit, can be known only *a posteriori,* after the judgment, and the individual is at the mercy of the judge.

This is the dark side of revolutionary justice in periods of terror. Even when such partisan tribunals are not a pretext for venting personal rancor and cloaking private vengeance with authority, it is still doubtful that they can really be considered organs of justice rather than bloody instruments of civil war. We in Italy have also had a recent bitter experience with revolutionary justice, and the same can be said of France. In fact, the magazine *Esprit,* one of the leading exponents of the spiritual values of Europe, felt it necessary to devote a special issue to this problem, in which Emmanuel Mounier anxiously poses the question, "*Y a-t-il une justice politique?*" Can there exist a political justice without there being a *contradictio in adiecto,* and how can a justice that is based on political criteria continue to be just?[7]

But in preference to this theory of judge-made law, this dynamic and romantic justice, the constitutional systems based on the separation of powers favor the static and "rationalized" theory of the legislative formulation of law, which claims to achieve the complete separation of justice from politics.

In the theory of the judicial formulation of law the passage from the field of politics to the decision is immediate and direct. The judge is immersed in politics. In the theory of the legislative formulation of law, that is, of the rule of law, the law lies between the politician and the judge. Law is still a product of

[7] *Esprit* (Paris), XV (August 1947).

politics, but in a refined and crystallized form. This refining process is carried on in two stages, a legislative stage, followed by a judicial stage. Like a rushing torrent pushing against a millwheel, all the political pressures are brought to bear on the legislative organs; it is the function of parliament to resolve these conflicting pressures into law. In his work of transforming politics into law, the legislator does not have in mind any specific incident that has already occurred. He operates on a plane higher than the individual conflict. From his aloof position he assesses collective interests and follows the direction and movement of social forces. And from this social diagnosis, based on generalities rather than on the individual case, he reaches the conclusion that certain typical modes of behavior are likely to lead to certain conflicts of interest, and therefore determines in advance, in a general and hypothetical manner, the just solution of all future conflicts having the characteristics of the type he has considered in the abstract.

An example of this can be seen in the legislation resulting from the housing shortage that occurred all over Europe as a result of the war. Parliament took note that a state of emergency existed, in which conflicts of interest between landlords and tenants had become a matter of public concern, and consequently it enacted legislation for the uniform regulation of all future conflicts of this nature.

The juridical system can be compared to a series of pigeonholes, in which each article of the codes is a separate compartment, made for a particular type of human conduct. All of man's actions that are socially relevant in a particular society are classified according to type and filed in the proper pigeonhole. Whatever has not been provided against has no social relevance, since the law by definition has no lacunae.

One can easily see how simple the second phase, the act of

judging, is according to this theory. As soon as the fact has been presented to him, the judge has only to find its proper juridical classification, that is, to recognize in it the typical characteristics of one of the models already placed in their respective pigeon-holes. Once the proper compartment is found, the judge has only to read the appropriate solution that has already been prepared.

This is the famous judicial syllogism, according to which the law is a general hypothetical judgment that joins a juridical effect to a future event: "If an act of type A occurs, it will produce juridical effect B." All the judge has to do is to certify that an act has occurred with the characteristics of type A, and that therefore juridical effect B should follow. The work of the judge is reduced to finding the coincidence between the concrete event and the abstract hypothesis as stated in the law.

You can see how rarefied and emotionally undemanding the work of the judge is from this point of view. He is protected from the crudities and impurities of politics, with which he has no direct contact; for between him and the political world there rises the impenetrable wall of the law. He has before him only the golden drops of logic of which each little legal syllogism is composed, and he is not aware of all the mud that had to be removed in order to find this precious ore, nor all the fire needed to purify it.

This is the theory of the rule of law, the perfect mechanism designed to operate in the happy periods of constitutional government. The theory is based on a serene optimism, where free play is given to all the illuministic principles of democracy, such as the "rationalization" of power, which protects the judicial decision from the influence of the judge's caprice; the separation of powers, which draws a line between the legislative and the judicial functions; and the certainty of the law, which is the basic protection of individual liberty.

We see in what an ingenious way this theory achieves impartiality. Parliament is impartial, since it deals in future generalities and cannot foresee which individuals will fall under the provisions of its laws, who will be the winner and who the loser, or which flesh and blood creatures will be placed in the compartments it has devised. And for his part the judge cannot help being impartial, because in judging he refers only to the law. According to this theory a just decision is not necessarily one in conformity with public opinion; it is simply a decision in conformity with the law. And if it should happen that the law is not in agreement, or is no longer in agreement, with public opinion, under the maxim *dura lex sed lex* this is not a problem for the judge but rather for parliament.

By this reasoning the decision is a product of pure logic, in which sentiment does not enter. The judge is able to live in the astral serenity of syllogisms, immune to emotional disturbances. Do you remember Montesquieu's famous sentence? *"Les juges ne sont que la bouche qui prononce les paroles de la loi, des êtres inanimés qui n'en peuvent modérer ni la force, ni la rigueur."*[3] They are inanimate beings, syllogizing machines, or better, they are optical machines. According to the panlogistic conception of the legal theorists, in virtue of the hypothetical and prospective nature of the law, that causes a specific juridical effect automatically to follow the occurrence of a certain predescribed type of event, laws apply themselves, descending from above to regulate the world; and thus jural relations, rights, and obligations are born, live, and die by themselves in the world of law without any necessity for the judge to intervene.

We all know that by syllogizing we jurists have created a world of our own where we imagine that we see living jural relations

[3] Charles de Sécondat, Baron Montesquieu, *De l'esprit des lois,* Livre XI, ch. 6.

as if they were animals of a metaphysical zoology, which only the initiated can observe. Just as Galileo pictured the universe as made up of triangles, we see rights strolling down the paths of our world, and we watch the baptismal and funeral ceremonies of jural relations. All this occurs without the judge being able to do anything about it; he is limited to the role of a spectator who observes what is going on and affirms its existence. He does not create rights; he merely certifies them. He is a mechanism made of special lenses, that enable him to see what already exists but is hidden from the naked eye; or rather, he is a projector whose beam of light reveals the mysterious submarine life of juridical organisms.

At this point I am tempted to ask a question of those of you who as judges or as lawyers have had practical experience in how justice actually functions. This is my question: Do you really believe that this purely intellectual and syllogistic conception of the judge is satisfactory, and particularly, do you think it is true?

The certainty of law. . . . Everyone knows in advance what his rights and duties are. Everyone can read in the laws, as on a price list, the legal cost of his future actions; any person who is able to reason at all can foresee his fate when he goes before the judge.

But is this reality or illusion? Is it true that under the rule of law the decision of the judge is predictable beyond possibility of error? Is it true that the judge, like a historian of judicial reality, merely ascertains what already exists without seeking to effect the practical expression of this reality by the influence of his will as it is stimulated by his emotions?

In a youthful study of mine[9] I too described the decision as a chain of syllogisms. Since then, however, my experience at the bar has shown that although not erroneous, that description is incom-

[9] Piero Calamandrei, "La genesi logica della sentenza civile," in Calamandrei, *Studi,* Vol. I, pp. 1ff.

plete and two-dimensional. The person who compares a decision to a syllogism does not see the decision as a living reality; he observes only its desiccated outer form.

Let us admit it, at least among ourselves. Who among us lawyers can predict the outcome of a case with certainty? Doubtless under the rule of law one has a better chance of making the correct prediction than under other conditions; particularly where provisions of a rigid and formal nature are concerned, such as statutes of limitations, or rules on estoppels, it is possible to predict the outcome of a case with a high degree of accuracy.

But even in these circumstances absolute certainty can never be attained. To the client who wants an assurance that his case will be won, the sober and honest attorney can only reply with the old proverb *habent sua sidera lites* (lawsuits go according to the stars). I once despised this proverb and rebelled against it, considering it a cowardly expression of base resignation.[10] When a man knows he is right, he should be confident that justice is more powerful than the adverse stars. With the passing of the years, however, I have become reconciled to the proverb, which, although it may have a discouraging effect on the attorney if resorted to before the case has been decided, may serve as a consolation after the decision has been reached. One must plan for victory and do one's best to win; but if the decision of the judge belies the lawyer's hopes, then is the moment to seek comfort in the wisdom of this Latin saying. The decision is unjust; no matter, we console ourselves with the thought, *habent sua sidera lites*.

But the judge is not actually a mechanism, a calculating machine. He is a living man, and the function of determining the law and applying it in a concrete instance, which in theory can

---

[10] Piero Calamandrei, *Elogio dei giudici, scritto da un avvocato* (2d ed.; Firenze: Felice Le Monnier, 1938), p. 3. (English edition, *Eulogy of Judges,* Princeton University Press, 1942, p. 3.)

be represented as a syllogism, is in reality a synthetic operation that mysteriously takes place in the sealed crucible of the spirit, where intuition and sentiment must be heated in an active conscience to solder together the abstract law and the concrete fact. The theory of the rule of law, and the normative theory of law in general, is an oversimplification, useful to jurists for didactic purposes, but such a logical breakdown of the decision is like a chemical analysis, which, even after identifying all the elements of which a living organism is composed, is still unable to isolate the spark that arises from the mysterious combination of these elements and gives them life.

Even under the rule of law, moreover, the laws themselves may afford the judge the loophole through which sentiment may be introduced into the rigid formulae that reason has dictated. Sometimes the law empowers the judge to decide according to equity, "according to the circumstances," or by "taking into consideration the specific circumstances of the case" (e.g., Article 2056 of the Civil Code). The language of the law often uses traditional expressions incapable of precise definition, like "good faith" and "due care," which have imaginatively been called the respiratory organs or the safety valves of the legal system, because by giving these elastic phrases a concrete meaning to fit the case at hand the judge succeeds in resuscitating the dead laws with the vivifying air of constantly changing social needs. But even without considering these technical expedients, by means of which the lawmaker consciously permits the oxygen of the irrational to enter rationalized law, we must persuade ourselves that in every interpretation of the law there is a re-creation, and individual inspiration is the decisive factor.

The pre-established law is one of the factors that stimulate the mind of the judge, but it is not the only one. This explains a certain lack of uniformity in decisions that would otherwise be incomprehensible. Two judges in two rooms of the same court building, even on the same day, can apply the same law to two identical cases and give diametrically opposite decisions. Which of them is wrong? Neither—because though the law was the same for both of them, though the facts were identical, the individual feelings of the judges through which that law and those facts were brought together were different. In cases like these there is nothing to do but acknowledge the power of *sua sidera*. The litigant who lost the case because he appeared before one judge would have won it had he gone next door. The judge is not to be blamed for giving a wrong decision; the litigant is at fault for choosing the wrong door. Even the ancient jurists were aware of the perplexity in which the judge finds himself when the point of law is so subtle and uncertain that the merest touch of sentiment is enough to turn the scales one way or the other; and they called this imperceptible influence the *"punto dell'amico"* ("friendship factor").[11]

We can therefore conclude by saying that to reduce the function of the judge to the mere act of syllogizing would impoverish, desiccate, and debase his noble profession. Justice is the creation of an alert and sensitive human conscience, and there must be an awareness of his responsibility for perfecting the law through the contribution of his vitality and his humanity.

The gravest danger that judges face in a democracy, along with most other public officials, is that of indifference, bureaucratic insensitiveness, and anonymous irresponsibility. For the bureaucrat men cease to be living persons; they become file numbers, index cards, and "cases"; that is, a folder full of papers, wherein is con-

---

[11] Giuseppe Salvioli, *Storia del diritto italiano* (9th ed.; Torino: U.T.E.T., 1930), p. 123, speaks of the "friendship factor" and traces it to Decianus. See Decius Tiberius Decianus, *Responsa*, Vol. III, Venetiis, MDCII, responsa LIX, No. 6, fo. 149: *"Amicitia facit iudicium pro reo, sicut inimicitia facit iudicium contra reum."*

cealed a desiccated man. The troubles of the living man who awaits official action no longer matter to the bureaucrat. He sees only the cumbersome file on his desk, and his sole concern is to find some expedient for transferring it to the desk of another bureaucrat, thus relieving himself of all further annoyance.

Woe to us if judges should ever become affected by this bureaucratic indifference, if they should ever become insensitive to the urgent call of their responsibility!

When one considers the weight of human grief that is borne by judges he may well wonder how they manage to sleep nights under this awful responsibility. And still, if the theory of the rule of law is interpreted literally, it might appear that the ingenious device of the judicial syllogism was designed expressly to relieve the judge of the weight of this heavy burden and to enable him to enjoy the innocent sleep of a child.

Let us suppose that a man is hanging in the square, condemned to death by the judge. The sentence has been carried out, although it was unjust; the man was innocent.

Who is responsible for the murder of this innocent man—the legislator who wrote the law establishing the principle of the death penalty, or the judge who applied it in this instance?

The legal syllogism offers both the legislator and the judge the opportunity to disclaim responsibility.

The legislator says, "I am not responsible for this death; I can sleep peacefully. The judgment is a syllogism, of which I am only responsible for the major premise, which is merely an innocuous hypothesis, general and abstract, threatening everybody but harming no one. The judge is the murderer; it is he who has derived the noxious conclusion from the harmless premises, the *lex specialis* that ordered the death of an innocent man."

But the judge replies, "I am not responsible for this death; I too can sleep in peace. The judgment is a syllogism, from which

I have merely derived the conclusion that logically results from the legislator's premise. The legislator is the murderer; his law was a *sententia generalis* that had already condemned an innocent man."

Lex specialis, sententia generalis—with these expressions the legislator and the judge disclaim their own responsibility and throw the blame on each other; in this way they are both able to sleep soundly, while an innocent man swings from the gallows.

But this cannot be the justice of a democracy; this cannot be the judge worthy of a community of free men. It has been said, as I have remarked previously, that democracy is a commitment, an *engagement: "faute de cet engagement la technique constitutionnelle est morte."*

The same can be said for the judicial technique.

We are no longer content with Montesquieu's judges, *"êtres inanimés"* made of pure logic. We want judges with souls, judges who are dedicated, who, aware of the constant vigilance and humanity required of them, accept the heavy burden and the awful responsibility of rendering justice.

III. *Independence and the Sense of Responsibility of the Judge*

THE LAST CHAPTER concluded with the observation that in a democratic society the judge cannot function like an adding machine, which gives the right answer if one presses the right buttons; rather, the judge as a moral person must be totally absorbed in the difficult mission of rendering justice and must be ready to bear the entire responsibility of the decision, which is not the product of an arithmetic operation but the result of a moral choice.

In saying this I do not intend to imply that the judge may disregard the law; under the rule of law the judge may not go beyond the limits set by the system itself. What I mean is that he should not consider the law an extraneous imposition coming from on high, but he must find its justification in his own conscience, and when he is about to transform the general rule into a specific command this command must be consonant with his own feelings. It has been said that a work of art is *"une tranche de vie,"* a piece of reality, reflected through the sensibility of an artist; it could as well be said that a judicial decision is a law filtered through the conscience of a judge.

In a democratic society the law expresses (or should express) a desire that is alive in the consciences of all its members, and the judge, who is the official interpreter of that law, must find in himself the reflection of the social conscience from which the law is born; he must read in his own conscience the general purposes that his people proposed to achieve by the law. But in order to dedicate himself wholeheartedly to this delicate searching introspection and to feel the full weight and the full honor of his responsibility, the judge must be *independent*. Only when he is alone with his conscience can he hear the still small voice of the law.

All modern democratic constitutions proclaim the independence of judges and of the judiciary, and consider this independence an essential guarantee of justice. In totalitarian regimes the judge is not independent; he is a political organ, a *strumentum regni*. The independence of judges can be realized in full only in democracies based on the principle of the separation of powers. The Italian constitution proclaims this independence in two articles: "Judges are subject only to the law" (Art. 101); "The judiciary constitutes an autonomous order, independent of all other powers" (Art. 104).

But what is the exact meaning of independence? What is the relation between an independent *judiciary*, one that is autonomous with respect to the other powers of the state (Art. 104), and an independent *judge*, one who in the process of reaching a decision receives no other commands than those of the law as it is revealed to him by his conscience (Art. 101)?

These concepts are coordinate but distinct. An independent judiciary, by which is understood a system of organs, established as an "autonomous order, independent of all other powers" and entrusted with the function of adjudication, is only a means (one of the means) of assuring the independence of the individual judge when he is deciding the case. The ultimate goal toward which all improvements in the judicial order must aspire is the independence of the individual judge, because if this is lacking, the judge cannot have that sense of moral responsibility which is the highest virtue of the magistrate.

The independent judge is, first of all, a judge free from all selfish motives while he is deciding a case. It has been said that in applying the law, the judge must revivify it in the warmth of his own conscience; but in thus re-creating the law, which is not an act of pure logic, the judge must regard himself only as a social man, participant in and interpreter of the society in which he lives. He must not be influenced to decide in favor of one party rather than the other by personal motives, such as ties of friendship or kinship, favors received, vengeance, fear of reprisal, or desire for money and honors—in short, all those things that Guicciardini would have called *"il suo particolare"* (his selfish interests). When he is deciding a case the conscience of the judge should be like a blank page on which the episodes of his private life have left no mark; his extra-judicial knowledge and experience may be present only if they lose their episodic significance and assume a broader and more serene social significance, thus turning themselves into "maxims of experience"[1] and becoming part of his general culture. The robe and the wig are symbols of this transformation of a private citizen into a judge, a person in whom individual sentiment may legitimately operate only as a function of his social mission as a judge.

It is obviously difficult for the judge to free himself from the net of personal ties in which his affections and private interests envelop him, particularly since it is often difficult for him to recognize them as selfish interests. While deciding the case he must forget that he is a husband or father; he must cease to think of his own economic straits or of the illness that saps his strength. The heroism of the judge can be measured by his degree of success in escaping from the prison of his private life; in spite of an inadequate salary that condemns his family to poverty he must

[1] Piero Calamandrei, "Per la definizione del fatto notorio," in *Studi*, Vol. II, pp. 289ff.

protect the unlimited riches of others without envy and according to justice; even when his father's heart may urgently call him to the bedside of an ailing son, he must remain in the courtroom to listen to the prolix arguments of attorneys; and in a trial for legal separation he must, if justice requires it, be ready to decide against the husband even if in his own marital life he has been unhappy but blameless.

It is difficult for the judge to check his private life outside the door before entering the courtroom, and it is especially difficult for him to distinguish within himself the personal prejudices and preconceived sympathies that seek to disguise themselves under a cloak of impartiality. Although the judge must not become an automaton and must always remain a human being, he is also required to put aside his private life. In all legal systems there are laws that are intended to help the judge free himself from his selfish interests, some of which go so far as to compel him, under circumstances where his ability to achieve impartiality is seriously in doubt, to disqualify himself so that another judge less prejudiced than he may take his place (Arts. 51ff., Code of Civil Procedure).

Generally, however, it is freedom from hierarchic control that one has particularly in mind in speaking of the independence of the judge. When he decides a case, the judge has no one over him empowered to give him orders or instructions. He cannot lessen his responsibility by hiding behind the authority of hierarchic superiors. He is bound by the law, but the meaning of the law that binds him he himself must determine according to his conscience.

Where there exists in the judicial order a hierarchy for purposes of appeal, a subsequent re-examination of the decision before a higher judge is made possible, but it does not lead to an obligation on the part of the lower judge to conform to the instructions of the higher judge in deciding the case. The most humble *conciliatore* on the lowest rung of the judicial ladder receives no orders when he is giving judgment, not even from the top magistrate of the hierarchy, the chief justice of the Court of Cassation.

An administrative official who fails to do his duty is not hard put to it to justify himself. He can always excuse his laziness or his negligence by blaming his limited powers of discretion. "I am only following instructions," he says, and shrugs his shoulders. But the judge receives no instructions when he decides a case. It is as if he were at the top of the pyramid, alone with the law and with his conscience, *superiorem non recognoscens.* From this point of view the independence of the judge could almost be considered a kind of sovereignty. His position is that of a sovereign organ, as is that of the members of parliament, who exercise their power "uninstructed" (Art. 67 of the Constitution).

But this freedom from all hierarchic control, which is easy to talk about, is difficult to achieve in practice, particularly in a parliamentary democracy. The solution of this problem is difficult and complex.

In a parliamentary democracy, parliament, as the representative of the sovereign people, exercises its political control over all the activities of the government. Each minister is responsible before parliament for the proper functioning of that branch of the public administration which he directs, and in order to keep his position he must retain the confidence of parliament. This is the principle of "ministerial responsibility."

The administration of justice is a branch of public administration, at the head of which is the Minister of Justice, who, like his ministerial colleagues, is responsible before parliament for the proper functioning of his own ministry—in this case, of the judicial system. And if he is to be responsible for its proper functioning he must have the organizing and disciplinary powers that are indispensable for maintaining or increasing the efficiency of the service, for correcting its weaknesses, and for suppressing its abuses. It is therefore imperative that the Minister have effective control over the activities and the discipline of the judicial organs. Control over the judges by the Minister, however, necessarily implies dependence of the judges on the Minister.

As long as this system is in effect the principle of the independence of the judiciary, of an "autonomous order independent of all other powers," cannot be realized. The judiciary cannot be autonomous so long as it is considered a branch of the administration, under the control of the Minister of Justice, and, through him, of the government.

In the present system there is thus a conflict between two principles, and this conflict is reflected in the personal insecurity of each judge. It is true that in the act of passing sentence the judge is performing a sovereign function and takes orders from no superior, but it is also true that the judge is a public official employed by the state and bound to it in a master–servant relationship, with a right to a salary and with corresponding obligations. Two qualities that appear incompatible are thus united in the same person—the constitutional independence of the function and the administrative dependence of the functionary. The judge, who as a sovereign organ is free of any hierarchic control in the act of judging, as an employee of the state is subject to the discipline of the service that employs him, which is headed by the Minister of Justice.

The danger in this hybrid system is evident. Whenever a politically significant trial takes place, the Minister, who is a political figure, may be tempted to influence or actually to limit the independence of the judges through his disciplinary control over them as his administrative subordinates and the power he has over their future careers. The judge is of course free under the law to decide a case according to the dictates of his conscience; but if the Minister or his political supporters discreetly call to the judge's attention the fact that his decision in a certain trial may be a determining factor in bringing about a hoped-for promotion or an undesirable transfer, there will again arise in the mind of the judge those disturbing influences of a private nature to which an employee who is concerned about salary and the cost of his children's education cannot remain indifferent. Nor can it be objected that according to the Constitution (Art. 107), "judges are not removable," and promotions must be made according to merit; in reality, as long as the judge is in fact a subordinate official in the Ministry of Justice, numerous ways remain open through which politics, by veiled threats and implied promises, may bring its disturbing influence to bear on justice. The danger is increased by the fact that lawyers may become members of parliament; thus the public is led to suspect that in certain trials the prestige of the attorney can be increased in the eyes of the judges by his political influence and affiliations. Notorious examples of this occurred during the Fascist regime when, as soon as a new Minister of Justice was appointed, those of his nearest relatives who had the good fortune to be lawyers, regardless of their mediocrity or their obscurity became overnight forensic luminaries and were besieged by prospective clients.

In preparing the new Italian constitution the Constitutional Assembly sought to remedy this situation by freeing the judiciary from all executive control and by providing it with a system of self-government. In order to effect the complete separation of the executive and judicial branches the suggestion was even made to abolish the post of Minister of Justice. Such a Draconian proposal might well have been complemented by a measure prohibiting lawyers from becoming members of parliament.

Although action of neither kind was taken, the principle of self-government was established, and all acts concerning the nomination, promotion, and transfer of judges, as well as disciplinary measures, which were formerly the responsibility of the Ministry of Justice, are now to emanate from a body called the Superior Judicial Council, which is headed by the President of the Republic and composed for the most part of judges elected by the judges themselves. The post of Minister of Justice, however, has not been abolished, and since the Minister continues to be politically responsible before parliament for the proper functioning of the administration of justice, he still retains the authority to initiate disciplinary action against the judges (Art. 107); and although his power in this respect is more limited than formerly, the fact that some of it remains is proof that he still has a certain administrative control over them (Art. 110).

Notwithstanding the fact that the constitution went into effect in 1948, the new law on the organization of the judiciary is still before parliament. Here parliament is faced with the difficult problem of reconciling the theory of a self-governing judiciary with the theory of ministerial responsibility.[2]

Even if the problem of granting the judiciary complete independence from executive control were to be satisfactorily resolved, and all acts relative to the legal status and discipline of judges were to emanate from a completely autonomous Superior Judicial Council, the freedom of the individual judge might still be insufficiently protected; even if the judiciary, operating as an autonomous constitutional power, were no longer in any way subject to executive control (Art. 104), this alone would not free the individual judge from problems of a personal and family nature that would still arise from his status as an official, dependent on

[2] This problem has been carefully studied in Italy in recent years. See *Sul Consiglio Superiore della Magistratura, Quaderno V*, of the *Associazione fra gli studiosi del processo civile*, Milano, 1953.

his salary for his livelihood and naturally desirous of promotion and economic advancement.

In the Italian judicial system, and generally in the judicial systems of continental Europe, the office of judge is not a *munus publicum* of a temporary and elective nature, like that of deputy in parliament, which is not (or should not be) confused with one's vocation; rather, it is a profession, for which the judge, in exchange for his full-time work, receives the means of his subsistence through his salary as a public official. The professional status of judges from the administrative and economic point of view, therefore, does not greatly differ from that of other types of civil servants; like them, the judges are part of a so-called "career" service, to which the official is appointed as a young man at the lowest grade of the hierarchy and through which he slowly rises to positions of increasing importance and to higher salary brackets. Only when he nears the termination of his career does the judge attain to the positions of highest honor and greatest remuneration.

The major subconscious anxiety of the judge, as of other salaried workers, is likely to be an anxiety over the success of his career. This becomes an obsession in those critical periods of his official life when he is eligible for promotion. Thus the judge may be influenced by his bureaucratic environment to think that the best way to render justice is to do what best advances his career. Since his chances of promotion will depend on the decision of a commission of higher magistrates who will evaluate his qualifications (which will be judged primarily on the opinions he has written), it is only natural that as the time approaches when he is to come up for promotion he will be led to neglect those phases of his profession that offer little opportunity for recognition but are of basic importance to the service of justice (e.g., the work of the examining magistrate in criminal cases), and to give preference to the type of work that enables him to make the most favorable impression on his future examiners. It is for this reason that judges who are nearing promotion tend to display their knowledge of jurisprudence by writing decisions as if they were preparing scholarly dissertations; for they know that to a promotion committee a learned decision is worth more than a just one.

We may therefore conclude that even when the time comes that the judiciary is freed of all executive control, it will still be possible for the independence of the individual judge to be endangered by his personal desire not to antagonize those upon whom the success of his career depends. If at that time the judge no longer shows his political complaisance by conforming to the views of the Minister of Justice, there may nevertheless remain a professional complaisance deferent to the views of the higher judges; and even if under the new system (as the Constitution provides, Art. 98), the judges are to be prohibited from openly belonging to political parties, nonetheless it is easily predictable that the elections to the Superior Judicial Council will lead to the formation *sub rosa* of competing political and religious factions, and that so as not to jeopardize his future career the judge who is awaiting promotion will seek to conform to the wishes of the dominant faction in the Council. In order to assure the independence of the judge the ideal remedy, which the English system approaches, is to abolish promotions and to give all judges, regardless of rank, similar honors and equal salaries, so that, once appointed to office on the basis of technical qualifications, the judge may remain there for the rest of his life, *quamdiu bene se gesserit,* free from that conformism that is the bastard son born of the union of fear and hope.

There are other aspects of the problem of the independence, and therefore of the responsibility, of the judge. One of the more important of these concerns the functioning of the plural bench.

When a single judge is empowered to decide a case, the entire responsibility for the decision falls on him. It bears his name; his is all the credit, and all the blame; and his sense of duty is increased by his isolation. But when, as often happens in Italy, the bench is composed of more than one judge and the decision is reached in conference behind closed doors, the consequent divided authority naturally tends to lessen the sense of individual responsibility of each judge for the decision, which gives the impression of being a unanimous opinion and therefore of having a certain degree of anonymity.

Just as the judicial syllogism may serve as a pretext permitting the judge to hold parliament responsible for his decision, so the plural bench may serve for each of its members as a convenient screen, shielding his conscience from the weight of an unjust decision and permitting him to cloak with a certain anonymity his agreement to a decision for which he would be unwilling to assume full responsibility.

But this problem has two aspects. If on the one hand the plural bench may act as a sedative for the judge and relieve his pangs of conscience for having committed an injustice, with the excuse that it was not committed by him alone (one might say that psychologically the plural bench leads to something similar to complicity), from another point of view the plural bench may become a defense of independence, since in certain politically important cases, where justice requires a decision against the wishes of the executive or the interests of the dominant party, the court may have need of a certain courage in order to overcome the temptation to seek personal advantage through conformism, and this courage may more easily be found in a plural bench than in a single judge.

In such cases it may be that, meeting in the secrecy of their chambers, the judges will be able to bolster up one anothers' courage.

The problem of the plural bench is closely related to that of the public or private nature of the deliberation. In Italy, although it is a fundamental rule that the trial be public, the decision in both civil and criminal cases is reached in private. At the close of the trial, after the presiding judge has pronounced the ritual, "The court adjourns to deliberate," the judges rise and disappear through the small door in the rear. What they say there to each other in private is not for outsiders to know. When they reappear in the courtroom the decision that is announced is their collective will. If there have been dissenting voices or scruples of conscience, no trace of them remains; they have been buried by the secrecy imposed upon what is said in chambers. The majority decision becomes, as it were, a unanimous decision, the impersonal will of the bench, not that of its individual members.

Undoubtedly there remains in this rite of secrecy something of the mystic aura that in the past surrounded the response of the judge—the voice of the Sibyl (as I mentioned in the first chapter), which came from above, not associated with any human form. For this reason in certain ancient drawings Justice is depicted with her eyes bandaged, less that she may not see than to create for herself the illusion that she is not seen.

But it may well be asked if the traditional secrecy of the judges' chambers actually serves justice, and if in the long run in a democratic society it is the public or the secret discussion of the decision that best serves to maintain the independence of the judge and to foster his sense of responsibility.

A similar problem arises in the field of parliamentary procedure, where voting may be open or secret. In the Italian procedure two forms of open voting are used, the rising vote and the roll call, while the method for secret voting is to deposit a black or a white ball in an urn. There is disagreement as to which is more consonant with the liberty of opinion and the sense of responsibility that are the bases of any democracy—the open vote, which requires the deputy publicly to assume responsibility for his political behavior, or the secret vote, which liberates him from the tyranny of party discipline and permits him to listen more freely to the dictates of his conscience. Under Fascism, in that ridiculous parody of a parliamentary assembly called the Chamber of Guilds and Fasces, only open voting was allowed; the "national councilors" were expected to say yes in a manly voice while raising their arm in the Roman salute; secret dissents had no place in an assembly composed of a tyrant's slaves.[3]

In the present Italian constitution votes of confidence must always be by a roll-call vote (Art. 94). Here the publicly recorded vote is intended to increase the sense of responsibility of the deputy, so that in a vote on which the fate of a ministry may depend the deputy must make his choice openly and accept his share of the responsibility for the consequences that may follow from this choice.

My own parliamentary experience leads me to believe, however, that even in a democratic system, where there is more than one party, the open vote may often serve to deaden the conscience of the individual deputy. I was present at the Chamber of Deputies during a two-day debate on the proper voting procedure to adopt. It was a question of deciding whether a certain vote required a roll call, which was the government's position, or a secret vote, as the opposition groups contended. This seemed to be purely a question of procedure, but actually it was a matter of considerable political substance. If the vote had been secret many members of the majority party would probably have voted against

---

[3] Law of January 19, 1939, No. 129, which created the Chamber of Guilds and Fasces, Art. 15: "Voting will always take place in an open manner."

the government and perhaps caused its fall; with open voting, however, the deputies of the majority party lacked the courage to vote against their leaders and the government was saved.

This goes to show that deputies vote differently according to the method of voting used; the method adopted thus controls the outcome of the vote. And since deputies and judges are made in the same human mold, this may also hold true for the decisions of the judges on a plural bench.

The secrecy of the discussion in the judges' chambers is traditional in the Italian judicial system, but it is not the universally accepted procedure.

In some countries, although the discussion of the decision takes place behind closed doors, the dissenting judges are permitted to express their opinion, which is included in the court records along with the majority opinion; and in the United States a judge who agrees with the decision of the majority but does not accept the reasoning by which it is supported may write a concurring opinion that arrives at the same conclusion by another line of reasoning.[4]

An outstanding example of this procedure is the Mexican practice. I had the privilege of watching its operation in an imposing session of the Supreme Court, which I had the great honor to be invited to attend. The discussion of the decision in this highest judicial body of the Mexican Republic, whose members have the title of Minister, takes place in public with a solemnity that could be called parliamentary. In a courtroom filled with spectators the presiding judge invites the reporting judge to read the draft of the decision that he has prepared and then opens the discussion on this draft. This discussion, which the public follows with great interest, takes place in the courtroom among the members

---

[4] See John Clarke Adams, *Il diritto costituzionale americano* (Firenze: La Nuova Italia, 1954), ch. III, Sec. 4.

of the Court, who speak in turn. It terminates with the final reply of the reporting judge, and then each judge announces his vote. If the majority is in favor of the reporting judge's draft, this draft is immediately proclaimed the decision of the Court. Otherwise a new reporting judge is appointed who will present a new draft at a future session. The lawyers, who have already presented their written briefs, take no part in this discussion; the only participants are the eloquent and learned judges who must decide the case. This procedure clearly requires that every judge make a careful study of every case so as to be able to discuss it in open assembly, for as each judge expresses his opinion he becomes responsible for it before the parties and the general public.

This system also has its weaknesses, which have been authoritatively discussed by Mexican scholars;[5] but on the other hand I have the impression that no less serious dangers can be encountered in the Italian system, which imposes complete secrecy on the judges' discussions in chambers.

In a country like Italy, in fact, where it is especially important to fight mental laziness and conformism even among the judges, our type of procedure is likely to aggravate the defects that it should eliminate. Particularly when the presiding judge is of an authoritarian disposition and is wont to cut short every expression of dissent in chambers, a judge might be encouraged to express and defend an opinion that he believes is just if he knew that his voice would reach the public and perhaps call forth a sympathetic echo; but if his opinion is destined to remain unheard beyond the secrecy of the judges' chambers, it is to be feared that in order to avoid fruitless argument with his superior (on whose approval sooner or later his promotion may depend) the dissenting judge

[5] See R. de Pina, *Temas de derecho procesal* (2d ed.; Mexico, 1951), pp. 101–108.

will prefer to keep silent and thus adjust himself to the expedient use of conformist behavior.

In the Italian procedure, however, there is no exception to the rule that imposes secrecy on discussions in the judges' chambers. The judge who reveals his opinion in any way during the trial before pronouncing sentence is guilty of an impropriety that may even expose him to disciplinary sanctions. In Italian practice the judge must remain as mute and inscrutable as a sphinx during the entire trial; even a smile might be considered an infringement upon the majesty of the office.

This system, however, is in contrast with the modern principles of oral proceedings, which must above all else be based on the direct collaboration between the judge and the lawyers, on the spontaneity of their relations, on their mutual confidence, and on the interchange of questions and answers between persons who seek in this manner to reach the truth. The tendency of the Italian judge to isolate himself in an impenetrable silence often serves to lengthen the legal process; the lawyer who speaks before an inscrutable judge, who controls even his gestures so as not to betray his thoughts, is forced to speak blindly, at the risk of expatiating on arguments of which the listener is already convinced, and of failing to answer objections that puzzle the listener, but which he carefully avoids formulating in words.

Certain traditionally minded judges believe that they are obliged to assume the impassible solemnity of idols while in court in order the better to maintain their dignity and authority before the lawyers. Thus they place a veil of incomprehension and arrogance between counsel and themselves. But fortunately, even in our country, there is an increasing number of courageous judges who realize the necessity of breaking down this barrier of distrust and taking an active part in the trial, not hesitating to interrupt and question counsel in the middle of his argument, to state ob-

jections, and to keep him from wandering from the essential issues
of the case. These are the judges who truly understand the modern requirements of their profession, and the lawyers should be
particularly grateful to these men, who dare to break the monastic
rule of silence in order to transform the trial from a pointless
soliloquy of a rhetorician before a dozing audience into a dialogue
between judges and counsel, who seek to understand and convince each other.

In order that judicial institutions may be adequate to the requirements of a free society, the traditional cloistering of judges
must end and instead the judicial process must be characterized
by a relationship between judges and lawyers expressing that
feeling of confidence, solidarity, and humanity which in all fields
is ever the animating spirit of democracy.

Among the most treasured memories of my long experience as
a lawyer there is that of an appellate court justice, now dead,
who after forty years of continuous service as a judge confessed to
me that in giving judgment he still felt the same sense of trepida-
tion that he experienced when he was first admitted to the bench
and prepared for the ordeal of deciding his first case. Forty years
of judicial experience had confirmed in him the belief that justice
does not mean insensitivity, that in order to be just the judge
need not be without pity. Justice entails understanding; and the
most direct way to understand men is to approach them with
sympathy.

Once this judge presided over a criminal appeal, the case of a
servant who had been accused of stealing a piece of silverware.
Although she had been acquitted by the lower court, the prosecuting attorney had appealed, and now in his summation before
the appellate court he was directing violent invective against the
accused, who was seated in the dock, silently crying. At a certain
point the judge called an usher and spoke to him in a low voice;

the usher then went over to the accused and whispered something in her ear, and she dried her eyes and stopped crying.

The spectators who noticed this incident were not aware of its significance, but when the trial was over and the court had adjourned to discuss the case, an onlooker asked the usher what the judge had said to him. He replied, "He told me to tell that woman to stop crying, because she was going to be acquitted."

In communicating his decision during the trial this judge violated the secrecy of the judges' chambers, but he respected the law of compassion, which forbids prolonging the grief of the innocent out of Pharisaic deference to cruel formalities.

IV. *The Crisis in the Reasoned Opinion*

THE MOST important and most typical indication of the rationality of the judicial function is the reasoned opinion. In all modern codes of procedure, whether civil or criminal, a reasoned opinion is prescribed as one of the requisites of the decision. The person who is interested only in the logical aspect of the decision finds the statement of the premises of the syllogism in the reasoned opinion and the conclusion of the syllogism in the judgment. The requirement that there be a reasoned opinion is considered so important in Italy that it has been placed in the Constitution, where it is stated that "all judicial acts must be reasoned" (Art. 111).

The major function of the reasoned opinion is an explanatory or, one might say, a pedagogical one. No longer content merely to command, to proclaim a *sic volo, sic iubeo* from his high bench, the judge descends to the level of the parties, and although still commanding, seeks to impress them with the reasonableness of the command. The reasoned opinion is above all the justification of the decision and as such it attempts to be as persuasive as it can. Ever since justice descended from heaven to earth and the idea gained ground that the judge is a human being and not a supernatural and infallible oracle to be adored, whose authority is beyond question, man has felt the need of a rational explanation to give validity to the word of the judge. And the reasoned opinion is precisely that part of the decision that serves to demonstrate the justice of the decision, and to persuade the losing party that the judgment against him was the inevitable conclusion of a logical process and not the result of oppressive and arbitrary improvisations. Even counsel for the losing party may find in the reasoned opinion the arguments that had previously escaped his attention and that convince him of the error of the position he had sustained. In this way losing a case after coming to the conclusion that it was justly lost is almost as satisfying as winning a case when we are convinced that the right is on our side.

But besides this psychological function of justification and persuasion the reasoned opinion has a more strictly juridical use, that of enabling the parties to determine whether or not there may lie within the reasoning on which the judge bases his decision any of those defects that make the decision susceptible to revision on appeal.

In the majority of cases the various appeals that the losing party may bring, before either the same or a higher court, are based on some error or omission constituting a departure from the logical *iter* followed by the judge, leading him astray and causing him to reach a mistaken conclusion in the judgment, that is, a conclusion other than the just one. Now the reasoned opinion, which is the written account of the issues of fact and of law that have led the judge to his conclusion (one might almost call it the log of his logical journey), is indispensable as a means of introducing the reader into the thought processes of the judge, of enabling him to ascertain whether or not at some point in his chain of syllogisms there is an error or a missing link. The reasoned opinion might be called a mirror that reveals the errors of the judge. When a lawyer studies a decision in search of grounds for appeal, he pays particular attention to the reasoning, dissecting its every paragraph, sentence by sentence, word by word, because there he may find hidden in a single word or grammatical construction a minute break in the logical continuity into which can be inserted the blade of appeal that may bring down the whole edifice. The importance of the reasoning as grounds for appeal is shown by the fact that in Italian law, as well as in that of other countries, any omission, insufficiency, or contradiction in the opinion concerning a point at issue may be sufficient grounds for quashing the judgment, whether the objection is raised in appellant's brief or is adduced by the reviewing court (Code of Civil Procedure, Art. 360, No. 5).

Reasoned opinions and appellate review are in a certain sense parallel institutions in the laws of procedure. As a general rule, where a reasoned opinion is not required, no appellate review is provided; for an appeal presupposes a criticism and a censure of the act appealed against, and this is hardly possible when the reasons and the justification for the act are not stated.

For this reason the decisions of the Courts of Assizes were final as long as the jury system was in effect in Italy. Since the verdict of the jury was not reasoned it could not be criticized, and therefore the decision based on such verdict was not appealable. The jurors replied yes or no to the questions put to them by the presiding judge, and the reasoning behind their answers was never made public. Unlike the judge, they were not required to seek to encase in cold syllogisms the impulses of sentiment, which, rather than reason, are often the basis of the decision. The unreasoned verdict of the jury, however, determined only questions of fact and their criminal classification. It was the task of the judge to assign the proper punishment for the facts ascertained and classified by the jury, in this way integrating the decision by supplying the essential elements not found in the verdict, and he was required to give the reasoning for his findings. Thus the reasoning was necessarily limited to the question of the punishment to be applied, and only within this narrow field was the decision susceptible to appeal.

The jury system was abolished in Italy by the Fascist regime, primarily for political reasons, because it appeared to be one of those institutions inspired by the nineteenth-century doctrine of popular sovereignty, anathema to the Fascist dictatorship; and in place of the jury system, in which the decision is formulated in two chronologically distinct steps, through the joint efforts of two different bodies operating independently,[1] a single body with mixed membership was formed, composed of regular judges and so-called assessors, whose decisions were required to be reasoned on questions of fact and of law, according to the regular rules.

The jury system was not re-established after the fall of Fascism. Although the political factors that led to its abolition were no longer valid, there remained technical reasons that counseled against its reintroduction. The present Constitution has re-established the principle of the "direct participation of the people in the administration of justice" (Art. 102); but since according to Article 111 of the same Constitution all judicial decisions without exception must include a reasoned opinion, it has been held that this unqualified constitutional provision prevents the reintroduction of the unreasoned jury verdict. Thus the decisions of the Courts of Assizes must be fully reasoned today in fact and in law, and appeal is granted against any part of them.[2] Perhaps this was a wise move, since the traditional jury system, in which the jurors were called on to judge without giving the reasons for their verdict, seems to have been fashioned—as

[1] Piero Calamandrei, "La sentenza soggettivamente complessa," in *Studi*, Vol. II, p. 211.

[2] Law of April 10, 1951, No. 287, on the reorganization of procedure in Assizes (modified by the laws of November 24, 1951, No. 1324, and of May 5, 1952, No. 405).

experience has borne out—for the very purpose of encouraging the jurors to judge unreasonably; and so, rather than the faithful expression of the social conscience, their verdict often appeared to be the triumph of pure irrationality, an irrationality that was all the more dangerous in that it was not susceptible to appeal.

The reasoned opinion seems to offer proof *per tabulas* of the essentially logical nature of the decision. One might say that even before it appeared in legal theory, the judicial syllogism was found in judicial reality, since the law requires that every decision be accompanied by a kind of logical X-ray that discloses its rational framework. One might almost say that in requiring the judgment to be preceded by the reasoning in the final form of the decision, it was the intention of the law to make evident the syllogistic structure of the decision and to persuade the parties in judgment that there was no room for arbitrary action in the inflexible concatenation of logical vertebrae.

Nevertheless some doubt arises when we consider the fact that according to the same laws of procedure, instead of being a *posterius* of the reasoning, the judgment is normally a *prius*. As an act of will the decision is already born before the judge has clearly expressed the logical process that has led him to decide as he did; the conclusion of the syllogism is thus irrevocably determined before its premises are formulated.

According to Article 274 of the Code of Civil Procedure, which regulates the discussion of the decision in the judges' chambers, "When the voting is finished, the presiding judge writes and signs the judgment. The opinion is then prepared by the *relatore*." Only after the opinion has been prepared can the decision be published (Code of Civil Procedure, Art. 133). And this may not occur until many days, sometimes many months, have passed after the decision has been reached. An even better example can be taken from criminal procedure, where the decision is announced at the close of the trial by the public reading of the judgment (Code of Criminal Procedure, Art. 472); while the complete opinion, including the reasoning that justifies it, is filed with the court clerk within a fortnight (Code of Criminal Procedure, Art. 151).

These laws leave us perplexed. Is the reasoned opinion really the logical premise from which the judgment is deduced as a necessary and inevitable consequence, or is it rather a kind of obligatory apology, by means of which the judge prepares ostensibly rational arguments in order to justify his decision in public, while his real motives are destined to remain hidden within his conscience?

The provisions of the laws of procedure mentioned above might lead us to suppose that the reasoned opinion is nothing other than a hypocritical expedient serving only, as it were, to give a logical disguise to an act impelled by quite different motives, perhaps even by arbitrariness and injustice.

These provisions are actually a candid recognition of the fact that the judge reaches his decision before he prepares the reasoned opinion; they are the clearest demonstration of the insufficiency and superficiality of those theories that reduce the decision to the form of a syllogism. In this instance the law itself is in contradiction to this theory. The accountant who attempted to determine the total before knowing the figures to be added would be ill advised; but, as I have already said, a judicial decision is no arithmetic operation. It is a far more complicated and mysterious act, rooted in moral consciousness and irreducible to numerical abstractions.

Rather than a preliminary study made by the judge to enable him to decide justly, the opinion is generally the expression of a soul-searching reappraisal made by the judge to convince himself that he has decided justly. Its purpose is to establish by logic the validity of a decision actually based on sentiment; it is the rationalization of the sense of justice, the demonstration of the *ratio scripta* that the judge prepares for his own peace of mind as much as for the parties, corroborating a discovery born of his intuition.

Even under the rule of law, when a judge decides a case he goes through basically much the same procedure as the lawyers do in pleading it. First comes intuition—one might almost say creative imagination—which suggests the thesis to sustain. Then comes the intellectual task of seeking legal grounds to support the thesis.

Those who have had experience in the legal profession know how the advice to give a client wishing to start a suit generally takes shape in the lawyer's mind (I am speaking of the honest lawyer, who realizes that he is his client's first judge): In first presenting his case to the lawyer the client lays before him an accumulation of disordered facts, from among which it is difficult to isolate the juridically relevant material. The lawyer sets himself patiently at the task of choosing, examining, and combining the separate pieces and of creating order out of the confusion. And finally there comes to him a flash of inspiration; that formless mass takes shape and acquires a significance, and in it there suddenly appears the outline of a familiar conformation, which gives juridical relevance to the case, much as Leonardo discerned human forms on walls cracked and discolored by dampness and age. Only after this relevance has been discovered, more through intuition than through reason, accompanied by an almost instinctive feeling of sympathy or repugnance, does the research work of consulting the law and the commentaries begin.

This "feeling" for the law is slowly acquired over years of practical experience at the bar. In its final stages it becomes a kind of clairvoyance. One of the happy moments in the life of a lawyer occurs when, thumbing through treatises and law reports, he finds the reasoned and rational confirmation of the correctness of the answer he reached intuitively through his "feeling" for the law. In this way he demonstrates that, rather than being a variable subjective illusion, the sense of justice, through a discipline of the spirit, is sharpened and perfected by experience so that the just solution, fully confirmed by the written commentaries, can be reached directly through intuition.

The uninitiated often believe that lawyers are omniscient beings who have memorized all the laws. How deserving of our pity lawyers would be were they expected to commit to memory the thousands of continually changing laws. But the lawyer is no legal handbook. He is the man who knows how to go about studying a case, who can discover what is juridically relevant in human problems, but above all he is the man who has a "feeling" for the just solution of a case. Often when one of my young assistants comes to ask my advice on a case he is preparing, I say to him, "I haven't studied the case and I don't know the pertinent law, but I *feel* that there *must be* a law setting forth this principle, or if there is no such law, there *must be* some legal precedent in this sense. . . ." I don't know the law and I haven't consulted the precedents; but when, after looking up the law on the points I suggested, my assistant comes to tell me that the provision I had imagined is actually to be found hidden in the labyrinth of special laws, or that in an old case book he has uncovered the very decision that confirms my diagnosis, mine is the same joy that the research worker in the laboratory experiences when his microscope gives him the empirical confirmation of the hypothesis suggested to him by his intuition.

Judges experience the same thing. For them the really decisive and culminating moment of their work is that of deciding the case; then if their legal sense is well developed the reasoning comes without effort. I have often heard judges who were called upon to decide a particularly complex and difficult case make the remark: "It is not hard to decide this case, but it is hard to give the reasoning." This explains the practice of the American courts, which not only permits dissenting opinions but allows the judges who concur in the judgment but not in the reasoning of the majority to write separate concurring opinions, basing the same conclusion on different grounds.[3] This practice shows that a given judgment is not necessarily derived from a given reasoning; even among the footpaths of logic it may be that more than one road leads to Rome.

Naturally, if in the actual process of judging, the reasoning follows the decision and is an explanation of it rather than a preparation for it, the reasoning may become a screen to hide the real factors on which the judgment is based, covering with plausible reasoning the true motives for the decision, which cannot be admitted. Once a German jurist made a painstaking analysis of many decisions to show that the reasons alleged in the opinion were not the real motives that had actually led to the decision. This was a subtle study of psychology and of judicial logic, the purpose of which was to reveal the true motives beneath the apparent ones.[4] The legal scholar with little experience in the courtroom reading the intricate reasoning of a decision as reported in a law review may often suspect, from the dialectical contortions and subtleties that the judge uses to justify his decision, that not even he was fully convinced by what he was writing, and that those arguments, couched in legal language, serve merely as a façade to hide from view the intrigue or partiality that was the true motivating factor of the decision.

[3] Adams, *op. cit.*, p. 27.
[4] Ludwig Bendix, *Die irrationalen Kräfte der zivilrechtlichen Urteilstätigkeit*, etc., Breslau, 1927.

In order to obtain the desirable fusion between the intuition that suggests the decision and the reasoning that verifies it (and consequently to make certain that the reasoned opinion be a true explanation and not a fallacious travesty of the decision), it is necessary that the judge's "feeling" and reasoning faculties be "in unison"; or rather that the same sentiment of social solidarity that inspired the legislators to enact the laws be alive in the mind of the judge to suggest to him the decision that his reason will later confirm. This is what is meant by such expressions as *ratio legis,* "the spirit of the law," "the intention of the legislator." In democratic regimes the law is a product of the social conscience. The legislator in a democratic state is not free to enact laws arbitrarily, disregarding the needs of society (although a tyrant or a dictator is free to do so for a certain period of time through the use of force); he must seek inspiration (and this is the purpose of the parliamentary system) from the collective conscience of the society that he represents. The judge is also part of the society in which he lives, and when he interprets the law in applying it to a specific case, he must draw inspiration from the same sentiment of social utility on which the law is based; to determine "the intention of the legislator" one must understand fully the significance and force of the law; this can be done only by turning for inspiration to the same social or political sources that inspired the legislator.

When it is said (and even I have been guilty of this) that under a government of laws the law is a wall separating the judge from politics,[5] only a half-truth is expressed, since a judge may be able to understand a law, interpret it faithfully, and feel in tune with it only by studying the political and social forces that created it. If a law is the result of a revolutionary change in government,

[5] Piero Calamandrei, "Processo e giustizia," in *Atti del Congresso Internazionale di diritto processuale civile.*

the judge who applies it cannot be guided by counterrevolutionary and reactionary sentiments. Under a government of laws the judge's sentiments must serve as a stimulus for integrating the law, not as an excuse for evading it, abusing it, or defeating its purpose.

At this point, if space permitted me to make more than a passing reference to this question, it would be fitting to evaluate the accuracy of those Marxist criticisms that make "bourgeois" justice the butt of their attack, understanding by this, justice as it is organized in the states of western Europe, administered by corps of legally trained judges appointed for life, claiming to be independent of any other power, whose sole function is faithfully to apply the laws that parliament enacts. It is not necessary to seek these criticisms in an orthodox Soviet source such as Vyshinski; it is sufficient to read the writings of Harold Laski,[6] an Englishman converted to Marxism, to find a demonstration that "bourgeois" justice is a "class" justice, in which the judge, like all other jurists, interprets laws enacted in the interest of wealth and privilege, and unconsciously becomes an instrument of this very tyranny, called on to justify by his subtle sophistry the selfish interests of the rich. In the struggle between the weak and the powerful that is at the core of Manzoni's immortal novel, *I promessi sposi,* the lawyer, Dr. Azzeccagarbugli, chose without hesitation the side of the powerful.

There is undoubtedly some truth in this criticism, not only because professionally trained jurists, who must have a university education that the sons of the poor are unable to afford, come from the so-called "bourgeois" class, but also because, if the law

[6] Harold J. Laski, *Democracy in Crisis* (Chapel Hill: University of North Carolina Press, 1933); Italian translation by Alessandro Schiavi, *Democrazia in crisi* (Bari: Laterza, 1935), pp. 118–127; and *Parliamentary Government in England* (London: Allen & Unwin, 1938); French translation, *Le gouvernement parlementaire en Angleterre* (Paris: Presses Universitaires, 1950), pp. 242ff.

is an expression of the interests of the ruling class, it is inevitable that the judge, if he wishes to be a faithful interpreter of this law, becomes an instrument of the same interests and thus, unconsciously, an instrument for maintaining that class in power. Since it is through the judge that the oppressed classes feel the oppression that is only abstract and potential in the law, they may be led to concentrate their animosity on the judge rather than on the distant legislator, for it is the judge who affects them directly, taking the threats that in the law appear remote and innocuous and transforming them into personal suffering. Public opinion often condemns the judge for the sin of the legislator; he is called a class judge, because he interprets class laws; in the allegorical paintings with which Orozco has adorned the Supreme Court building in Mexico City, one can clearly see what the enchained people thought of the judges serving an oppressive regime.

This accusation loses much of its value, however, when applied to the judicial organization of democratic parliamentary states; where, even though the judges are appointed for life and generally come from the middle class, the constitutional mechanism so operates as to permit a continual change in the ruling class and therefore of the interests that it protects by legislation. In this way the gradual adaptation to the new social requirements that occurs in legislation is inevitably reflected (and sometimes foreseen) in the decisions of the judges, where one can follow more clearly than in the laws the slow, laborious but uninterrupted progress of social justice.

It might also be observed that when Marxists accuse "bourgeois" justice of being an instrument of political struggle which the ruling class uses to maintain its favorable position, they make an accusation that, even if in part valid, can all the better be turned against them; because in the dictatorship of the proletariat justice is openly vaunted as a political weapon for the defense of socialism. The only difference is that although in the western system of a government of laws political pressure can affect the judge, before it reaches him it has been purified in passing through the filter of the law.

During periods of tranquillity and social stability, where a continuous peaceful social revolution obviates the necessity for abrupt changes, when the laws in effect are accepted by the majority as expressions of popular will, and the judge in applying them feels spiritually at one with the legislative voice of his people, the normal function of the reasoned opinion, which is to furnish a rational basis for the socially inspired feeling of justice that first prompted the judgment, is performed effectively and efficiently, in what might be called a physiological manner.

But the poignant potentialities of the reasoned opinion become apparent when the judge's sense of justice is not in harmony with that of the legislator; when as a result of abrupt political changes and a break in juridical continuity, the judge is called on to apply a law that he believes unjust. It is very well to say that under the rule of law the principle *dura lex sed lex* applies and that consequently the judge must take the law as he finds it, without judging it. But the judge is a human being, and as such he automatically judges the law before applying it; even if he is willing to obey it, he cannot avoid making a moral and political evaluation according to the dictates of his conscience. And even if he stifles the voice of his conscience, when he is obliged to apply a law in which he does not believe, it is only natural that he will apply it mechanically, as an official duty, with a cold bureaucratic pedantry; he cannot be expected to vivify or to recreate a law that is extraneous or actually hostile to his philosophy. When under these conditions the law is applied by a judge who does not approve of it and who is not in sympathy with the forces that gave it birth, it is reduced to a dry formula, to be applied literally.

It is on these occasions that those pathological conditions of conflict and disharmony occur between the judge and the law that cause the reasoned opinion to lose its physiological function and to become either a screen of studied hypocrisy designed to hide the true motives of the decision or a form of disguised protest, through which the judge, in the very act of formally deciding a case in accordance with the law, sees to it that by reading between the lines of the opinion that pretends to show the justice of the decision one can discover why the judge believes it unjust.

Then the crisis of legality, the cause of which is always a more or less acute incompatibility between the laws in effect and the needs of the society, takes the form of that singular phenomenon in judicial pathology that might be called "the crisis in the reasoned opinion."

Recently the causes of this crisis have been so numerous and have arisen from such varying sources that scholars have been able to distinguish and classify certain prevalent types much as if they were working in an experimental laboratory. In Italy, as elsewhere, this crisis has made itself felt repeatedly.

First of all, during the Fascist dictatorship and the German invasion there was the difficult moral decision to be made by the judges who were obliged by the foreign and domestic tyrants to apply cruel and senseless laws that were repugnant to their consciences (e.g., the so-called race laws persecuting the Jews). Even greater was the inner torment of the judges who in their official capacity were required to impose sentence for the violation of laws that as citizens they themselves were violating every day. I can never forget the pathetic case of a judge whose duty it was to sentence persons accused of buying food on the black market in violation of the rationing laws during the war, who every morning before coming to the court went the rounds of the city in frantic search of black market meat for his own sick child.

There has recently appeared in America a highly original study by Professor Cahn entitled *The Sense of Injustice,*[7] which, in order to demonstrate pragmatically how the sense of justice arises and operates in society and in the realm of law, focuses on its negative aspect, on that natural rebellion that is awakened in the human conscience in the face of injustice. Like the illness that makes us appreciate the health we had previously taken for granted, or like the air for which we feel a need only when we are deprived of it, so the sense of injustice reveals to us the value of justice at the moment we are in danger of losing it. In reaction to inhuman laws like those of "racial" persecution there welled up an irrepressible sense of injustice, stronger than reason, leading the judges to seek ingenious pretexts for not applying those abominable laws. The opinion was often the cleverly camouflaged screen behind which this noble treason was accomplished. A study of great political and social interest could be made in attempting to show by an analysis of their opinions the great efforts the judges made to limit the application of those odious laws, against which their consciences rebelled. Such a study would show the moral level of the judges in that period.

But in the countries where the war brought about the fall of the dictatorships and the return of liberty the crisis of the reasoned opinion has now reappeared in another and quite different form.

The fall of the Fascist regime did not lead to a radical change of personnel in the judiciary, nor to major changes in legislation. Even after the promulgation of the republican constitution most of the old laws remained in force, and the same judges applied

[7] Edmond N. Cahn, *The Sense of Injustice* (New York: New York University Press, 1949).

them who for twenty years had been accustomed to interpret them with a conformist spirit. In the long run habit becomes a form of sclerosis, for judges as well as for others. So long as the laws remain the same, even though the regime has fallen and the constitutional premises have been drastically changed, how can a judge who has grown old through twenty years of dictatorship be expected to interpret in a new democratic spirit the very laws that for twenty years he considered the expression of an authoritarian philosophy?

A judge who has not become irrevocably attached to the spirit of the old laws may have recourse to an evolutionary interpretation; in the elastic provisions of the laws that have remained apparently unchanged, a new spirit can enter through reference to the general principles of the new order. If only he is willing to take the trouble to raise his eyes from the Code before him and look for a moment out of the window at what is happening in the street, the interpreter can easily see that the significance of certain articles whose wording has not been changed is the exact opposite today of what it was under Fascism. For example, the crime of "subversive propaganda" (Art. 272 of the Criminal Code) actually means today quite the opposite of what it meant twenty years ago.

But not all judges are able to make this slight effort. Particularly those who have grown old in the service are likely to remain attached to the old fetishes. It is difficult, after having interpreted laws for twenty years according to one philosophy, to retain the mental agility necessary to break away from the old prejudices and adjust to the new philosophy. In the periods following an abrupt change, a strange assortment of illogical reasoning and of ill-assorted and incompatible conclusions may appear in the opinions of the judges: republican laws interpreted in a monarchist spirit, democratic laws interpreted in the Fascist spirit, laws designed to bring about innovations interpreted in a spirit of conservatism. In such cases the opinion is often at odds with the judgment and may even attempt to discredit it.

Theorists have long been aware of the so-called suicidal decisions,[8] in which the judge is careful to let it be known by his opinion that although he has resigned himself to deciding the case in a certain way in deference to the spirit of conformism, he is nevertheless fully convinced in his own mind that this decision is unjust. In this way in order to save his soul he exhorts his readers not to take his decision seriously and to try to have it reversed on appeal.

In the last ten years all countries whose legal systems have undergone basic changes have experienced other misuses of the reasoned opinion, such as in the polemic decisions where the opinion has been used by certain nostalgic judges not to state the legal reasoning on which the decision is based, but as a pamphlet suitable for a political rally, serving only as an outlet for partisan feeling.

And there are other still less savory subterfuges, like that of a judgment absolving the accused and that he therefore has no interest in appealing, which is followed by an opinion of an almost libelous nature, made public only after the time limit for an appeal has elapsed.

But these, fortunately, are exceptional cases, isolated symptoms of that *malaise* occurring during the period of readjustment after rapid social changes and inevitably affecting the judiciary.[9] Then gradually the old incorrigible judges retire, the younger judges who grew up in the new political atmosphere take their places, and there is established in the judiciary a harmonious relationship

[8] G. Escobedo, *Sentenze suicide*, Città di Castello, 1941.
[9] Piero Calamandrei, "La crisi della giustizia," in *La crisi del diritto*, Padova, 1953.

with the spirit of the new laws that had previously been lacking, and thus the "crisis in the reasoned opinion" is overcome.

We should not be discouraged. Merely because in periods of general social unrest judges also function less efficiently, we should not cease to have faith in justice.

A few years ago a French jurist, Georges Ripert, of the Law School of the University of Paris, wrote a book worthy of study, entitled *Le déclin du droit*, which sounded like a tocsin warning of the crisis in law from which Europe is suffering.[10] Ripert makes an acute and careful analysis of this crisis: The law of the strongest, the degeneration of private law into public law, the spirit of disobedience, the discontinuity of the law, the uncertainty of the law, the weakening of individual liberty. The conclusion of the eminent jurist is rather pessimistic: The law is declining. But, with all due respect for this learned scholar's understandable and touching concern, his conclusion calls to mind an epigram that I learned as a child in an elementary school book.

Sedeva in pianti e lai
la signorina al mar;
la commoveva assai
del sole il tramontar.

—Si calmi, signorina;
l'affare così va:
il sol di qua declina,
e torna su di là.—[11]

---

[10] Georges Ripert, *Le déclin du droit* (Paris: Librairie générale de droit et de jurisprudence, 1949).

[11] A little lady sat   "My lady, ease thy mind
  lamenting by the shore,   and conquer thy despair;
  deeply grievèd that   the sun that here declined
  she saw the sun no more.   will soon rise over there."

The law is like the sun; after its decline it will rise again. And if we want to fulfill our social duties we jurists must not lament the twilight of the old justice. It is much more to the point to see to it that, rather than being an instrument for conservation, the law becomes an instrument for peaceful social evolution, capable of forestalling new catastrophes and guiding the world toward the dawn of a new justice.

v. *The Dialectical Aspects of the Judicial Process*

AFTER having devoted three chapters to the protagonist of the procedural drama, the judge, it is now fitting that we should turn to the other indispensable personages in every judicial process, the parties, who, to continue the theatrical metaphor, should not be called the "antagonists" of the judge, since, though they are each other's antagonists, they are necessary collaborators for the judge, even if he is not always aware of this fact.

There are necessarily two parties in every judicial process. Even in the so-called ex parte proceedings the dialectical aspects of the process (which, as we shall soon see, are today one of its essential attributes) have required that in modern legal systems an official, or one might say an artificial, party be added. This happens in the criminal trial, where the prosecuting attorney opposes the accused, and it occurs in certain civil trials, as, for example, in cases to determine legal capacity. Here the only interest to be protected is that of the person whose legal capacity is in question. The law, however, requires the presence of a plaintiff to act against him.[1]

In the modern judicial process, which reflects the constitutional principles of modern democratic states, two parties are indispensable. The fundamental principle of the process, its motivat-

[1] Piero Calamandrei, "Linee fondamentali del processo civile inquisitorio," in *Studi*, Vol. II, pp. 321ff., and "Il processo inquisitorio e il processo civile," in *Ibid.*, Vol. V (1947), pp. 53ff.

ing force, the guarantee of its effectiveness, is the "principle of the judicial debate": *audiatur et altera pars; nemo potest inauditus damnari.* "The right of defense is guaranteed at every stage of the proceedings" (Constitution, Art. 24); "The judge cannot pronounce judgment on any claim if the opposing party is not present or has not been duly summoned" (Code of Civil Procedure, Art. 101).

The parties are *persons,* that is, subjects having rights and duties, and they stand not powerless before the judge, required to obey passively, but as free citizens who come before him not merely with obligations to fulfill, but also with rights to protect. And the judge is not only possessed of power over them but is a public servant, bound to them by duties and responsibilities, so that the parties have the right to express their opinions freely and to be heard with attention. The theory of the procedural relationship, each subtle phase of which has been illuminated by Giuseppe Chiovenda in a manner that has in my opinion withstood all the criticism directed against it, including that of James Goldschmidt,[2] is only a transformation, in the microcosm of the judicial process, of the general theory of the *Rechtsstaat,* of the modern state limited by law. Here the citizen is not a helpless object at the mercy of an absolute monarch; he is an autonomous person having rights and duties, whose autonomy is guaranteed by the law even in his relationship with the state itself; and as the constitutional order becomes increasingly democratic, the reciprocal rights and duties of the citizen versus the state become more definite and "rationalized."

Jural relations are relations *between persons.* When we say that the judicial process is a jural relation between the judge and the parties, there is an implicit recognition that the judge

[2] James Goldschmidt, *Der Prozess als Rechtslage,* Berlin, 1925, pp. 1–145.

is not the only person possessed of an independent and juridically relevant will, but that there are three such persons, the judge and the parties. This truth is expressed in the classical legal maxim: *processus est actus trium personarum.*

Therefore the judge is never the only actor in the judicial process. This process is not a monologue; it is a dialogue, a conversation, a give and take of proposals and answers, an interchange of actions and reactions, of attacks and counterattacks, of arguments and refutations. For this reason it has been compared to a sports competition,[3] except that it is a game of persuasion and argumentation, rather than of athletic prowess.

The *dialectical aspect* of the modern judicial process is its most precious and typical characteristic. It is the reason that the will of the judge is never absolutely sovereign, but is always conditioned (even in criminal procedure) by the will and behavior of the parties; that is, by their initiative, persuasiveness, resistance, and acquiescence. And the same can be said for each of the parties, for his will and his activity are molded and conditioned at every step of the process by the stimuli he receives from the behavior of the opposing party and the judge.

Except in this three-dimensional form, the modern type of judicial process cannot exist. One might say, paraphrasing an ancient maxim, that *tres personae faciunt processum.* In certain historical periods a type of judicial process has existed in which the judge was the only person whose will was effective. Until recently it was thought that this process was permanently buried in the past. Here the judge did not have before him free and responsible men prepared to defend themselves, but only unprotected victims, helpless before his unlimited arbitrary power and already condemned. Such was the process of the Inquisition,

[3] Piero Calamandrei, "Il processo come giuoco," *Rivista di diritto processuale* (1950), Sec. I, pp. 23ff.

where the functions of investigator, prosecutor, and judge were united in a single man, the inquisitor, before whom the accused was not a person but an inert object, a pitiful bundle of flesh, fit only to suffer torture and annihilation.

At a recent university gathering my friend Alcalà Zamora told us an amusing story of a trial that took place several centuries ago in Spain against the locusts. This is an example of a curious judicial practice that was also found in Italy, where there are records of criminal trials conducted against animals accused of crimes and solemnly condemned to death.[4]

The famous trial of the dog in the third act of Racine's *Les Plaideurs*, held in order to give the half-mad former judge the pleasure of trying him, is a burlesqued parody of this ancient aberration. But when trials against animals are held in all seriousness, as they were in certain historical periods, one can see under this curious practice an authoritarian conception of the judicial process that makes of the judge an absolute despot and the only actor. For such a judge man and beast are the same. He seeks no collaboration from the accused. He does not treat him as if he were endowed with the dignity and responsibility of a human being who is helping to determine his own fate; he sees before him only an inanimate object, whose earthly fate is already written in the mind of the judge, just as much as is that of the animal that the butcher weighs before slaughtering. This was the inquisitorial process, which we once thought had vanished with the age of barbarism, but which instead has recently reappeared in the guise of that frightful counterfeit of justice which in modern terminology could be called the "totalitarian" process. Here the parties are merely figurative elements that serve to increase the spectacular aspects of the rite, and the will of the judge is

[4] Carlo Lessona, *Giurisprudenza animalesca*, Città di Castello, 1906, pp. 39ff.

everything; and his decision, instead of being the final product of the judicial process, evolving from the contrast of opposing wills, and therefore uncertain and undetermined while the trial is in progress, is the arbitrary act of a single will, which stages the trial in order to give an illusory retrospective justification for a decision that has already been reached.

In the dialectical process the decision is the consequence of the trial and is not known until it is over; in the totalitarian process the progress of the trial is determined by the decision, *which is already settled before the trial begins.*

It is easy to find a certain parallel between the judicial process and the constitution of the state in which it operates. There still exist absolute authoritarian states, where the totalitarian type of judicial process is used, in which the judge is all-powerful and the parties before him are treated as things. And there are also liberal and democratic states, where the judicial process reflects the liberal and democratic structure of the state, just as a drop of water reflects the sky.

In a study of mine on the "relativity of action,"[5] I tried to show that the different attitudes with respect to the eternal struggle between liberty and authority that are accepted by various types of constitutions are reflected in variations in the concept of "action." But this relation between the judicial process and the constitution of the state in which it operates cannot be limited to the single concept of action; a comparison between the law of legal procedure and constitutional law, between the judicial system and the system of government, can be instructive and can open new horizons with respect to the study of the whole judicial process.

We are indebted to that great German proceduralist, James

[5] Piero Calamandrei, "La relatività del concetto di azione," in *Studi,* Vol. V, pp. 1ff.

Goldschmidt, sent to exile and death by the criminal and insane race persecution of his government, for pointing out the close relationship between the dialectic aspects of the judicial process and the political doctrine of liberalism. In the preface of his basic work, *Der Prozess als Rechtslage* (1925), we read that legal procedure can flourish only in the soil of liberalism. It is for this reason that in an article honoring his memory I called him "master of procedural liberalism."[6]

In reality, the dialectical aspects of the judicial process resemble those that operate in parliament. In a certain sense (and *cum grano salis*) the opposing parties in the judicial battle do not function differently from the opposing political parties in parliament. The same principle of initiative and responsibility, which when applied to the parties in litigation goes under the name of the "dispositive principle," by virtue of which either party in a civil process may bring about his own victory by the soundness of his reasoning and by his ability to express it (*faber est suae quisque fortunae*), has many points of similarity with the dialectical aspects of parliamentary procedure, where each political party may bring about its own victory at the polls and may rise to power through the soundness of its program (and alas! through the cleverness of its propaganda). Democracy is a dynamic form of government, continually striving for its own success. It is animated by the constant desire to improve itself and to outdo the opposing groups in the quality of its programs and in their effective persuasiveness.

The debate between the opposing parties in court is as like as two drops of water to the debate between the government and the opposition in parliament. Both systems are based on ideas that are so simple as to appear naive: that men are reasonable

---

[6] Piero Calamandrei, "Un maestro di liberalismo processuale," in *Rivista di diritto processuale* (1951), Sec. I, pp. 1ff.

beings, able to persuade others of the correctness of their own ideas, and equally able to be persuaded by the correctness of the ideas of others; that the whole truth can be known only if it is studied from various points of view by circling around it to find its three dimensions; and that the antagonist is a collaborator, not an enemy, because by his objections he helps to uncover and correct errors and to foster that competitive spirit that leads to greater human progress. In the British parliamentary system, as is well known, there is an organized and responsible opposition, which is considered a necessary organ of good government. In fact, "Her Majesty's loyal opposition" is so much appreciated that its leader receives an official salary almost equal to that of the Prime Minister, and sits at the same table with the Government, facing the ministers and on the same level with them.

In the same way the opposing party is indispensable in the judicial process; not because he increases the animosity and belligerence between the parties and not because he permits counsel to give vent to greater eloquence, but in the interest of justice and the judge, for whom the best and easiest method of seeing the whole truth before him, illuminated from all sides, is through the juxtaposition of the opposing claims of the parties.

This comparison between the judicial process, based on the opposition of two parties, and the parliamentary system, founded on the struggle between the majority and the opposition, has more than a purely theoretical value; that is, the similarity is more than purely aesthetic. During the final years of the Nazi domination, proposals for reforming the law of civil procedure were discussed in Germany (and if the regime had not fallen, these proposals would certainly have been enacted into law in a ruthlessly logical manner), by which it was planned to abolish the freedom of the parties and to transform the *Parteiprozess* into a procedure where all initiative would emanate from the judge.

They even used the term "a trial without parties," which is equivalent to saying "a trial without a trial." One eager student[7] even discovered that the concept of *Parteiprozess* was a malignant virus that had infected the bloodstream of justice and that had originated in those partisan hatreds that afflicted Italy in the time of the city states, when political life was a free-for-all among the warring factions. But since finally (according to this scholar) the totalitarian Nazi state had happily succeeded in freeing political life from factions by arranging that all conflicts would be resolved within the paternal breast of the *Führer,* it was now incumbent on them to eliminate the parties in the judicial process and thus bring to bear the cult of the *Führerprinzip* on the judicial system, so that there would be heard in the courtroom only the sacred pronouncements of the officiating judge, before whom the persons in judgment wait silently, prostrate and adoring.

If in a democracy the judicial process ought to be a civilized discussion among equals, it is easy to see the importance of lawyers to the democratic legal order, for they are the necessary interlocutors in such a dialogue. The outcome of the judicial process and therefore the fate of justice depend on the friendly and fair progress of the discussion. The proper functioning of justice depends less on the soundness of the law than on the good relations among judges and lawyers.

I pointed out in the first chapter that *judicial practice* is more important than the law in assuring the proper functioning of the judicial process. The creators of this practice are the judges and the lawyers; they mold it with their morality, their behavior, and their comprehension. In the judicial process judges and lawyers are like a system of intercommunicating vessels; the level of culture and good faith remains the same for both groups, rising

[7] Piero Calamandrei, "La crisi del processo civile in Germania," in *Studi,* Vol. V, pp. 285ff.

and falling at the same rate. Good judges make good lawyers and vice versa. Judges who despise counsel despise themselves, and lawyers who fail to respect the dignity of the bench offend the dignity of the bar.

Sometimes the "obligation of honesty and good faith" is placed on the parties and their counsel by law (Art. 88, Code of Civil Procedure), but the law is silent and must always remain so with respect to the real meaning of this obligation. Good faith and honesty must reside in the conscience of both judges and lawyers. It is custom that counts; respect for the rules of the game cannot be imposed on persons who do not feel it, but nevertheless this respect is as essential in the judicial process as it is in parliament. For this reason the disciplinary power that the professional associations exercise over their members has great importance in the legal profession; the surveillance over the good faith and honesty of lawyers and over the observance of the unwritten rules of accepted behavior must come *from within,* from the very conscience and sense of responsibility of the bar association, autonomous and self-disciplined.

For this reason the transformation of the bar from a free profession to a state bureaucracy would mean the end of its usefulness, and of justice as well. Twice in history this transformation has been attempted—in the Prussia of Frederick the Great and in the Russia of Lenin;[8] and both times the experiment attempted by such different types of authoritarian states failed, and in order to save justice it was necessary to return to a free bar, or at least, as in Russia, to grant the parties the right to choose their own paid counsel.[9]

In the judicial process the lawyers represent freedom; they

[8] Piero Calamandrei, *Troppi avvocati,* Firenze, 1921, pp. 25ff.
[9] Piero Calamandrei, "Gli avvocati nel mondo," in *Rivista di procedura civile* (1926), Sec. I, p. 327; "Libri sugli avvocati," in *Rivista di procedura civile* (1930), Sec. I, p. 350.

are the living symbol of what is perhaps the vital principle of modern democracy: that to attain justice one must take the road of freedom; that freedom is the indispensable instrument for attaining a greater justice. In the first years of the Fascist terror, when the *squadristi* were going about on their punitive expeditions, the objects of their destruction were not only the labor union headquarters and the public libraries, but also lawyers' offices. In Florence, toward the end of 1924, more than twenty lawyers' offices were sacked and burned in a single day. This is not surprising. The lawyer is a danger for dictators; he is the symbol of critical reasoning, of rebellious opposition to all conformism; in regimes of oppression and moral degradation the last refuge of freedom is the bar. When all others are silent and crushed under tyranny there still come from the bar occasional acts of dignity and courage.

The course of the judicial process is governed by the judicial practice created through the collaboration of judges and counsel. According to their desire for accomplishment or their concern with personal convenience they can accelerate or retard it.

It is useless for the laws of procedure to set deadlines and limits if judges and lawyers are unable to agree among themselves on a balance between the lawyer's duty to protect his client and his equally important duty to be a loyal collaborator of the judge, and not to impede the course of justice by the use of delaying tactics. If judges and lawyers alike fall into the comfortable habit of dilatory procedures, it is in vain that the codes prescribe time limits, prohibit postponements and establish summary proceedings.

The history of legal procedure offers many examples of how judicial practice has condoned these fatal delaying tactics, which make a mockery of the laws of procedure, particularly when applied to the very provisions that were enacted for the express purpose of speeding up the process. Every time the legislature has tried to eliminate some of the stultifying ceremony of the regular so-called formal proceedings by creating special abbreviated summary proceedings for the most urgent cases, within a period of a few years judicial practice has succeeded in slowing down and formalizing this procedure, the justification of which was its supposed celerity and simplicity. This curious phenomenon (which with an ugly but apt neologism was called the "desummarization of summary procedure") periodically occurs in history; when a summary procedure comes in contact with judicial practice it tends to become formalized and to take on itself all the delays and complications of the ordinary process. It would almost seem that instead of being grateful to parliament for trying to make their work easier and less encumbered with formalities, lawyers and judges were agreed on trying to defeat every attempt at accelerating the course of judicial proceedings.

There is a confirmation of this in the law of July 14, 1950, No. 581, modifying the Code of Civil Procedure of 1940. It should be noted that these modifications were made on the recommendation of the lawyers. All of these modifications, including those that abolished or limited certain estoppels (Art. 184), or that admitted appeals against rules of practice that had previously been final (Art. 178, Code of Civil Procedure), or that permitted an immediate appeal of an interlocutory order (Art. 339), have necessarily resulted in slowing down and complicating the legal process, even if this was not the intention of those who suggested the changes.

The slowness of the judicial process, of which everyone complains in Italy, is not a phenomenon that can be attributed solely to extraneous causes, such as the general regression brought about in all branches of public administration in the past decade as a result of the war. Its causes are more deeply rooted in judicial practice. The excessive complications of the proceedings, and the insistence on meticulous observation of senseless formalities, could easily be kept within bounds if a greater degree of mutual trust existed between judges and lawyers. *It is distrust that retards and complicates the judicial process.*

If we compare the administration of justice in England with that of France and Italy, we must take into account a difference that at first sight seems quite incredible: the same judicial function that some 6,000 career judges are unable to perform effectively in Italy is accomplished successfully and with considerably greater rapidity in England by not more than 100 judges!

The true reason for the speed and simplicity of English justice, which seems almost a miracle to us, is the sense of loyal collaboration that unites lawyers and judges there, and that makes observation of procedural formalities generally superfluous. Many of the formal safeguards that are found in our procedure have been put there to assure a fair trial to both parties and to eliminate the unethical practices of dishonest litigants. This has been made necessary because of the mutual distrust that exists between the judge and the parties, as well as between the parties themselves. It is necessary to regulate all these matters in great detail in part because it is feared that if the law were not explicit, each party would try to take advantage of every procedural loophole to prevent his adversary from having a fair chance to defend himself; and also because it is feared that if the proceedings were not regulated by law an unsympathetic and unconscientious judge would use his discretionary power to bring the trial to a speedy close and thus free himself from the annoyance of listening to counsel.

Procedural ritual is similar to religious rites in that the formal complication of the liturgy is not necessarily an indication of a sincere faith. The numerous rules of procedure by which the law attempts to guarantee a fair trial are symptomatic of an unhealthy condition; when the law finds it necessary to impose fair methods of procedure, conscience is not doing its part.

In all types of social relations mutual trust is a simplifying agent, for trust means solidarity, sociability, understanding. The judicial process is no exception. The chicanery so highly valued by shyster lawyers is primarily responsible for the time-consuming complications of legal proceedings. It is from such chicanery that the *cautelae ad protrahendas causas ad longum* are born, which permit a case to drag on indefinitely, and it is from the fear of the use of chicanery by an unethical opponent that the provisions limiting postponements become necessary. But these counterbalancing formal safeguards are of little service so long as spiritual safeguards are lacking.

A typical example of how distrust can alter procedural regulations can be found in Article 180 of our Code of Civil Procedure. When the Code was put into effect in 1942, it read in part as follows: "The procedure before the examining magistrate is *always* oral." With the reform of 1950 the "always" was deleted. The article continues to say that the procedure is "oral," but the omission of "always" shows that it need not be so. In practice, even before the examining magistrate, oral procedure is falling into disuse. This phase of the process, which in the intent of parliament should be a confidential discussion between the lawyers and the judges, sitting around the same table, has again become, as under the old system, an interminable number of postponements voluntarily granted by the judge, that give the lawyers the opportunity to exchange an infinite succession of written briefs. The function of the examining magistrate is often reduced to that of registrar and grantor of requests for postponements. It seems that the judge prefers not to speak directly with counsel and thus simplify the case and clarify the essential issues. Even the lawyers prefer to present written briefs in formal legal style rather than to give their arguments orally in a simple and direct manner.

This failure of oral procedure and this bureaucratic crystallization of the examining magistrate is in part, at least, the result of the excessive work load with which the judges are burdened. In the most crowded judicial districts an examining magistrate has to handle a hundred cases or more simultaneously. Under these conditions it is easily understandable that he is unable to give each of them its due attention and is not in a position to discuss each case intelligently with defense counsel. For oral proceedings to be successful, both judges and counsel must be prepared to discuss the case. Written proceedings allow for delay and permit the judge and opposing counsel to study the case at a later date; and it is in part for this reason that both counsel and judges prefer the written procedure.

But the basic cause of this preference is distrust. Lawyers prefer not to disclose to the judge the arguments on which they base their defense, as would be necessary in an oral discussion; they do not want (and sometimes they are unable) to reply immediately in the presence of the judge to the objections of opposing counsel. In order to keep a trial in the form of a dialogue, in the course of which many kinds of unexpected questions may arise, it is necessary to prepare a case more thoroughly than is the habit with a number of lawyers; and they must be less suspicious that every move of the opposing counsel is a trap. Therefore they prefer to take their time to think things over carefully, to look up the law, and to reply in writing a fortnight later. The greatest enemy of oral proceedings is the fear of compromising oneself. It can even happen that the judge is afraid that he may reveal his decision prematurely if he discusses the case directly with counsel. He is afraid that the lawyers, particularly if they are able and widely respected, will succeed in misleading him by their persuasive eloquence. Even the judge is suspicious, and rather than hear the arguments of counsel, he prefers to read them and to meditate upon them in solitude.

Thus oral proceedings are doomed to failure because of distrust. Judge and counsel could get to the heart of the case immediately by sitting together around the same table with the court clerk ready to write down what they say, but they prefer to remain in each other's presence only long enough to set the date for the next meeting. They prefer to express in an exchange of written briefs what they might have said directly to each other. And in the same way the next hearing will serve only for obtaining a further postponement to enable the lawyers to prepare their replies. Thus the judicial process becomes an exercise in composition. The judge and counsel act like timid lovers who do not know what to say in each other's company but who, as soon as they are apart, compose long love letters, which they keep with them for several weeks, awaiting their next opportunity to exchange them in silence.

The method of selecting the judges may have a determining influence on the re-establishment of the mutual confidence between lawyers and judges that is an essential condition of a successful judicial process. If only persons who had practiced law for a number of years could be appointed judges, this past experience might be expected to aid them in understanding some of the problems that arise in defending clients and make them more tolerant of the acts of intemperance and exhibitions of stubbornness that defense counsel may show; and vice versa, if lawyers had had some experience on the bench before becoming practicing attorneys, they would better appreciate the difficulties and the moral strain inherent in the act of judging. For this reason I admire the British system of selecting judges, where the most famous and respected lawyers are appointed to the highest judicial offices, so that the bench is considered the continuation and the natural fulfillment of the lawyer's career. Lawyers and judges thus feel themselves united in a single fraternity; the attorney trusts the judges because only yesterday they, too, were lawyers like him; the judges trust the attorney because they know that tomorrow he may join them on the bench.

The relationship between lawyers and judges, which is the fundamental problem of the judicial process, is a problem of comprehension. The judge must understand and appreciate the degree to which his burden is lightened by the presence of counsel who take upon themselves the tiring labor of translating the raw facts of life into comprehensible legal language; but the lawyers must also understand that the judge's task is more grievous and challenging than theirs because, while the lawyer, like a soldier in a trench, knows beforehand from what direction the enemy will strike and where he must shoot, the judge must choose, and his alone is the awful responsibility of that choice.

To improve the relations between lawyers and judges, perhaps more than comprehension is needed. I venture to suggest that there must also be mutual charity—comprehension and charity even for the inevitable shortcomings and omissions that all men, judges as well as lawyers, are guilty of during their long day's labor.

I should not say that the judge who has already made his decision before the oral hearing in which counsel presents his case has given proof of charity and comprehension; for while counsel wears himself out at the trial, such a judge lets his mind wander and lulls himself to sleep by thinking of pleasanter things. The lawyer is a man, not a mechanism. Often he is an old and ill man. To speak in court is for him a trying experience for which he must marshal all his resources and spare himself nothing. If the judge is not pitiless, the call of human charity alone should be enough to require him to listen with attention.

But on his part the lawyer is guilty of an act of cruelty when he insists on inflicting his endless and pointless oratory on a long-suffering judge, worn out after a hard day of hearings and no longer able to listen attentively; or when instead of summarizing his brief in a few well-reasoned pages, he spreads his argument thinly through voluminous memoranda that fall on the hapless judge with the weight of tombstones.

Thus even in the relations between lawyers and judges we always return to the secret of any democratic success, that the relations must be among free men, each the guardian of his own independence and his own integrity, but at the same time aware of a social solidarity that unites them for a common purpose. In the judicial process judges and lawyers are like mirrors: each one as he faces the other recognizes and salutes the image of his own integrity.

VI. *Respect for the Individual in the Judicial Process*

WE HAVE already seen how the judicial process unfolds and develops through the dialectical opposition of three persons (the judge and the two parties before him), of three wills conscious of and responsible for their actions, how the trail leading to justice is discovered by following a route that at the moment of departure is unknown even to the judge. This road is not straight and at the start it is not clear where it leads; its direction is revealed step by step as the trial proceeds along the various twists and turns resulting from the interplay of the three wills—*di pensier in pensier, di monte in monte* (from thought to thought, from crest to crest), as Petrarch would say.

But in order to assure the effective functioning of this dialectical collaboration between judge and counsel, it is not enough for the two opposing parties to appear before the judge and for him to hear both their arguments; there must further exist a condition of equality between the parties, not merely legal equality (which may exist only in the abstract), but also effective equality, which means technical and economic equality.

Even in the administration of justice there is a real danger that the poor man will find himself at the same disadvantage that is his lot wherever the democratic system protects only his political and civil liberties, which are the common possession of all citizens. For the man who lacks the economic means necessary for making these liberties a reality, they are often nothing but an unfulfilled promise. "The law is the same for all" is a beautiful sentiment that warms the heart of the poor man when he sees it written on the wall of the courtroom, high over the heads of the judges, but when he discovers that to avail himself of his presumed equality he must spend more money than he can afford, the beautiful phrase becomes a sour jest, as if he had read on the wall that by virtue of the constitutional provision for freedom of the press (Art. 21) all citizens are equally free to publish a newspaper with a large circulation, or that by virtue of the provision granting freedom of education (Art. 34) all citizens are equally free to send their children to a university.

Again we meet that fundamental requirement of a true democracy that is expressed in the words "Justice and Liberty." This was the slogan that was written on the banners of the partisan brigades during the Italian resistance movement. If liberty is not to be an empty word, all citizens must at least start out with that minimum of social justice and financial means that will permit them to derive material benefit from their civil and political liberties.

The Italian Constitution pays lip service to this requirement when it states that every worker has the right to a wage "in every instance sufficient to provide a decent and free existence for himself and his family" (Art. 36), and more particularly when it states that "the Republic shall remove the obstacles of an economic and social nature that constitute a *de facto* limitation on the freedom and equality of citizens, thereby impeding the full development of the human personality and the effective participation of all workers in the political, economic, and social organization of the nation" (Art. 3).

This slogan, "Justice and Liberty," serves as an indispensable premise for the proper functioning of a trial. Doubtless the parties are theoretically equal in the civil process. In the criminal process not only are the arguments of the defense given equal weight with those of the prosecution, but according to the letter of the law, the accused is actually in a privileged position because until he is adjudged guilty there always remains a presumption of innocence in his favor (Constitution, Art. 27).

The equality of all citizens before the law, firmly established in the Constitution (Art. 3), finds its judicial complement in another article (24), providing that "everyone may act at law for the protection of his rights and legitimate interests" and that "the right of defense is guaranteed in every step of the proceedings." Thus the right of action in the abstract sense, that is, the right to seek justice from the judicial authorities, and the right to defend oneself are part of our constitutional law, part of the fundamental rights possessed by everyone, not only citizens but under certain circumstances by foreigners as well. This "constitutionalization" of the rights to equal treatment before the courts is a typical feature of modern constitutions.[1]

But of what practical importance are the equality of citizens before the law, the right of defense on conditions of equality with the opposing party, the right to action granted equally to rich and poor, all of which have been duly inscribed in the Constitution? In his famous *Kampf um's Recht*, Jhering does not consider the struggle to protect rights in the courtroom under the antisocial aspect of litigiousness, but on the high and noble plane of the defense of human dignity and social peace, which, requiring as it does an immediate reaction against every wrong through legal channels, cannot be safeguarded by cowardly acquiescence in wrongdoing. But again the question may be asked: Is every citizen in an economic condition to make this sentiment of civic pride productive of material benefits, or is the struggle for justice

[1] This subject is masterfully treated by Eduardo Couture in his *Las garantías constitucionales del proceso civil*, Buenos Aires, 1946.

often a luxury that the poor man cannot afford? The story of the miller of Sans Souci is well known. In answer to the threats of the sovereign he replied, *"Il y a des juges à Berlin."* This phrase honors the judges of Berlin in that it shows that they were not unworthy of the confidence of a poor man who might be involved in a lawsuit against a rich and powerful opponent. But these also are only words, because history has never explained what the miller could have done had he lacked the money to go to Berlin and retain a lawyer able to defend his interests before the court.

Thus even in the judicial process it may happen that in the language of the Constitution "obstacles of an economic and social nature . . . constitute a *de facto* limitation on the freedom and equality of citizens, thereby impeding the full development of the human personality . . ." (Art. 3). This suggests that in certain instances there may be no *de facto* equality between the parties corresponding to their *de iure* equality. Even though both parties have the same legal rights, the means at their disposal for availing themselves of these rights may be far from equal. In the judicial process, as well as elsewhere, inequality of means may be tantamount to inequality of legal personality.

Meanwhile it should be pointed out that the right to defend oneself, which is "guaranteed in every step of the proceedings," actually means little more than the right to counsel. The protection of the individual in the judicial process is not merely a question of protecting him from any acts of violence or intimidation that would deny or diminish his freedom to defend himself as he is able; it also implies that he is entitled to positive help in defending himself and in availing himself of those procedural safeguards that the law affords for this purpose.

Regardless of their legal equality, the parties often find themselves unequal in education and intelligence. Should they have to defend themselves, the less intelligent and less educated party would be at the mercy of the better educated and more experienced party; and in criminal proceedings the innocent man who was incapable of expounding the proof of his innocence with clarity would be more at the mercy of the prosecution than a guilty man relying on his experience and his cunning.

In the modern world the judicial process is a complicated technical mechanism that succeeds in becoming an instrument of justice only for those who know the secrets of its operation. This leads us to the conclusion that to assure the freedom and equality of the parties in the actual judicial process, at every step of the procedure each must be defended by an attorney who through his intelligence and his specialized knowledge of court procedure is able to establish a real equality between them. When faced with the intricacies of the judicial process the parties, untrained in judicial matters, are in a certain sense similar to persons lacking legal capacity. The relation between the client and his counsel is therefore similar to that between a ward and his guardian; the attorney is not only the agent of his client, but in a certain sense he supplements his client's legal capacity and acts as an integrator of his personality.

The presence of an attorney is therefore the most important indication of respect for the individual in the judicial process; where there is no attorney the personality of the party is diminished. In civil cases it has no protection against either the opponent's bad faith or the pitfalls of procedure, and in criminal cases it is in danger of being ignored because of the prosecution's position of overwhelming superiority.

The right to counsel, without which the right to defend oneself is of no practical meaning, does not exist during the first phase of the criminal process in those systems in which the pre-trial phase is carried out in secret without the presence of defense counsel. This is the phase in which the accused, alone and unde-fended before the examining magistrate, may be unable to find in his own innocence sufficient strength to resist the effects of prolonged questioning, and in order to put an end to his ordeal may be reduced to signing a confession to a crime he has not committed. Unfortunately, Italian criminal procedure retains this sad inheritance from an era of tyranny, which is unreconcilable with respect for the human personality; but since the present Constitution guarantees the right to defense "in every step of the proceedings" (Art. 24) the Code will have to be altered to permit the presence of defense counsel during the pre-trial phase.

But even when the presence of defense counsel shall be re-quired during the entire criminal process, there will still remain in both criminal and civil cases the problem of the defense of the poor. Here the Marxist criticisms are valid when they speak of justice made for the rich. The costs involved in presenting one's case in proper legal form are so high that not infrequently the poor man must endure the bitterness of suffering for the wrongs of those richer than he. Thus the right to a legal remedy, like freedom of the press or the right to an education, is in danger of remaining a luxury available only to the rich.

The problem of defending the poor, which is actually the problem of creating an effective equality between the parties in the judicial process, has not yet found a satisfactory solution; be-cause it depends on larger problems of an economic and social nature, it is possible that this solution cannot be found in the narrow technical field of judicial institutions.

Our Constitution states in the third paragraph of Article 24 that "The poor are guaranteed through the help of apposite institu-tions the means of seeking a legal remedy and of defending them-selves before any tribunal." But, in the case of damages for judicial errors provided for in the same article, this protection is more a promise than a reality.

In Italy the civil process is exceedingly expensive. The stamped paper on which all legal documents must be written, the court costs that lie in wait at every step of the procedure, the traditional fiscal practices[2] requiring the registration of affidavits presented in court and forcing the parties to burden the proceedings with oral testimony in an effort to escape these charges—all this complicates even the simplest cases and greatly increases their costs. There is also the lawyer's fee to be considered. Being a professional man who must make his own living, the lawyer has the right to an adequate remuneration.

In Italy free legal aid is organized as an "honorific and obligatory function of the legal profession."[3] In both civil and criminal cases a person who is unable to afford an attorney of his own choosing (the so-called *difensore di fiducia*) has a right under certain conditions to have legal counsel designated for him, and this counsel is obliged to serve without fees unless he wins the case and collects from the opposing party.

This system has its merits and its defects. Above all it relies on a spirit of sacrifice and sympathy toward the underdog, which is in the noble tradition of the bar; and many times this spirit is sufficient to assure the poor man the assistance of a zealous attorney. But it is inevitable that in assigning counsel the choice falls on the young lawyer with little to do, eager to accept even nonpaying clients, rather than on his distinguished and experienced colleague whose time is entirely taken up by his highly remunerative private practice. It may happen that the poor man will be fortunate enough to be defended by a neophyte filled

[2] Piero Calamandrei, "Il processo civile sotto l'incubo fiscale," in *Studi,* Vol. III, pp. 75ff.
[3] Royal Decree-Law, December 30, 1923, No. 3282.

with the sacred fire who puts his whole heart into the defense, but he may also have the misfortune to be saddled with a negligent and procrastinating attorney who fails to follow the prescribed procedures and who considers a poor man's cause an *experimentum in corpore vili.*

But this should not lead one to think that the poor man can never be defended by a first-rate attorney. More frequently than is generally believed famous lawyers are willing to serve the cause of justice by taking the case of a client who can pay them nothing, even if it means sacrificing a part of their lucrative practice; in spite of the fact that lawyers are persecuted by a reputation of rapaciousness, they do not always forget that their tradition also bestows on them the sacred privilege of serving widows and orphans, without thought of personal gain.

It used to be said *ianus advocati pulsanda pede*—one must knock at the lawyer's door with one's foot—because one's hands must be full of gifts. Renzo knew this when he went to the home of Dr. Azzeccagarbugli carrying his famous pair of capons.[4] But there have also been lawyers of a different stamp. At San Gemignano there is a fresco portraying Yves, Bishop of Chartres, practicing the profession of a lawyer; on one side are shown his rich clients in the antechamber with their arms full of expensive gifts, waiting vainly to be received; on the other side is shown the bishop's office, where he is seated in his chair lovingly counseling the poor, to whom he has given precedence. Even in the past, then, there were lawyers who considered it their mission to defend the just causes of the poor without seeking personal gain. In the name of historic truth, however, we must add that such cases were probably not very frequent, even in those times, since the case of Bishop Yves was considered a miracle by the people:

[4] Translator's note: The reference is to Alessandro Manzoni's historical novel *I promessi sposi.*

advocatus sed non latro, res miranda populo. In fact, he was made a saint after his death, and is the patron saint of lawyers.

The system of free legal aid adopted in Italy cannot really be considered entirely satisfactory, however, as, although providing the poor man with counsel, it denies him the chance to have an attorney of his own choosing, thus lessening the mutual trust, the most important and most satisfactory bond in the relationship between counsel and client. An outstanding judge, Pasquale Saraceno,[5] who had risen quickly to the rank of appellate court justice, and then was murdered on the threshold of his office just as Florence was being liberated, used to come to see me often in the preceding years of sorrow and anguish, and spend long hours discussing legal problems; at a time when our whole legal system seemed about to crumble about us in ruins, we sought to console each other by discussing abstract problems of constitutional law, and, in particular, those concerning the organization of the administration of justice in a democracy. Ours was a sort of *de consolatione iuris,* a companion piece to the *De consolatione philosophiae.*[6]

Saraceno looked upon the function of judge as if it were a religious mission. He told me once, seeming to ask my pardon for his bluntness, that he felt lawyers always had a disturbing and profane influence on this mission. The judge, he said, never has two equal parties before him, who permit him to weigh serenely in the balance the case presented by both sides; the two opposing lawyers pleading before him are rarely of equal ability, being dissimilar in eloquence, astuteness, learning, and experience. This inequality is even more apparent when one of the parties is rich

[5] Author of valuable studies in legal procedure, of which the most important is *La decisione sul fatto incerto nel processo penale,* Padova, 1940.

[6] Translator's note: The reference is to *The Consolation of Philosophy,* written by the Roman senator Boethius while in prison before being executed at the order of Theodoric in 525.

and the other poor; for the rich man monopolizes the best lawyers, and the poor man, if he is able to find counsel at all, must rely on a third-rate lawyer quite incapable of coping with the battery of able attorneys opposing him. Now all this disturbs the proper functioning of justice and leaves the judge with a feeling of discomfort and dissatisfaction. He is not always able to free himself from the influence of the illustrious attorney before him, nor can he himself make up for the omissions of the inexpert defense if the poor man's counsel is incompetent.

Saraceno concluded by saying that if we cannot forbid the rich to employ the best lawyers, it might be better, in order to preserve the equality of the parties, to eliminate lawyers altogether.

I have already explained why lawyers cannot be eliminated without making it practically impossible for judges to perform their functions. Were the bar to be dissolved, in the space of a few months the judges themselves would be clamoring for its re-establishment.

Nevertheless, to decrease the injustice that my friend deplored, caused by the inequality of counsel in cases between the rich and the poor, a system of free legal aid should be devised that would permit the poor contestant an opportunity equal to that of his rich adversary to be represented by a first-class lawyer of his own choosing.

Therefore the unqualified right of defense should not mean that second- or third-rate counsel will be appointed to defend the poor man but rather that he will be free to choose his own counsel. As long as the rich man has this choice, the poor man must have it also in order that an effective equality may be maintained between the parties in the judicial process.

The principle has already been established in the legislation of democratic countries that to lessen the conditions of economic inferiority of labor with respect to management in capitalistic societies, the state must intervene to establish an equilibrium between the parties. This is the principle from which springs the constitutional recognition of the right to strike (Art. 40).[7] The special procedure laid down for labor disputes and the creation of special bodies to settle them have the same purpose, which is to compensate for the position of inferiority of the poor man who is in conflict with a man richer than he. Labor unions serve this function when they make available to their members without cost the services of their own specialized legal staff.

But labor disputes are not the only type of dispute in which it may be necessary to establish economic equality between the parties. The problem of the poor man's defense is broader than this. Various methods have been proposed to solve it.[8] One suggestion is that the dispensing of free legal aid should be entrusted to the law schools, so that persons unable to pay could benefit from the counsel of the eminent lawyers teaching there, while the students could gain practical experience under the guidance of their professors much as they do in a medical clinic. But the success of this system would depend upon the cooperation of the professors and on their willingness to set aside their scholarly work and devote a portion of their time to such a clinic. Even under this system, however, the fate of the poor litigant would be determined by chance and not by his own free choice of counsel.

As long as the bar remains a free profession based on a relationship of trust between client and counsel, I believe that the ideal method of providing legal aid for the poor man so as not to put him at a disadvantage would be to permit him to choose his

[7] See Piero Calamandrei, "Significato costituzionale del diritto di sciopero," *Rivista giuridica del lavoro*, 1952.
[8] See Couture, *op. cit.*, p. 44.

own lawyer, who instead of being paid by the client would be paid by the state, or, better still, by the bar association, through the creation of a special fund set up for this purpose. But this system could not produce satisfactory results under present conditions, as in many European countries the excessive number of lawyers has produced a kind of "forensic proletariat" in need of cases, which would see in such a system only a means of attracting clients and fomenting litigation.

From this point of view the need of supplying the poor with legal counsel is part of a larger problem. It is another aspect of the crisis in the legal profession, which in turn is an indication of a general and profound social dysphoria.

Addressing myself to a western hemisphere audience, I am reminded of a little treatise in the form of a dialogue, written in Venice about 1560 by Francesco Sansovino, son of the great Iacopo Sansovino, who designed the *Procuratie,* the colonnades of the Piazza San Marco.[9] The father wished the son to become a lawyer, but after a short time the latter tired of this profession and started to publish the books that he had written on a wide variety of subjects. Among these is to be found this curious sketch of the Venetian bar, wherein he laments the fact that even then Venice was overrun by a mob of inferior lawyers without clients, and places the responsibility for this forensic decadence on none other than—Christopher Columbus. In this dialogue a certain Lorenzo has this to say:

> "Our forefathers, who were famous and worthy men, lived in times quite different from the present. Then maritime trade was the principal occupation, and was held in great honor; and young men were sent out to the Levant at an early age, where after making their fortunes they grew old in peace and comfort.

[9] Francesco Sansovino, *L'avvocato e il segretario,* Piero Calamandrei, ed. (Firenze: Le Monnier, 1942).

Since many young men emigrated, there were few lawyers, and those few were kept busy, as the great amount of commerce brought about much litigation. These lawyers, then, were highly esteemed and became wealthy, as in important cases they received high fees.

"But the contrary is true today, because ever since first Christopher Columbus and then the Portuguese discovered the new trade routes, which decreased the traffic passing through Venice, the young men, no longer finding opportunities in commerce, have turned to the law in the mistaken assumption that there would be as much legal work as in the past. The result is that before the older generation realized it, the decrease in trade and the increase in lawyers together produced a situation in which there were not enough cases to keep the lawyers busy."

Such was the reasoning of Francesco Sansovino. In upsetting the economic balance of the Old World, the discovery of America struck a fatal blow to the sober traditions of the Venetian bar. This would almost lead one to believe that the present crisis in the legal profession in Europe may be a result of broader economic problems besetting the world.

But aside from this still existing inequality of the poor man and the rich man before the court, it is certain that modern non-inquisitorial-type civil procedure is inspired throughout by a respect for and a desire to protect the integrity of the individual.

The motivating force of this procedure is responsibility. Even in the search for truth, the party, save in the exceptional instance of the *inspectio corporis,* is never the object of investigation, but rather is always a collaborator with the judge in setting the limits and supplying the means for this investigation. He is not obliged to appear in court nor to reply to questioning nor to tell the truth; his will is restrained by no binding obligation. He is free to behave as he sees fit; but he must remember that by failing to appear or to tell the truth, he is likely to bring about his own downfall.

This type of civil procedure leaves inviolate the personal sovereignty that every man preserves deep within his consciousness. The dialectical principle behind it is a continuous call to reason and to the sense of responsibility of the parties.

Thus when the parties and their counsel all act in good faith, the trial is a perfect example of orderly and respectful democratic collaboration.

But what a long road there is ahead of us before we will find any such respect for the individual in criminal procedure!

This is a terrifying subject that merits a long and painful commentary of its own. Here I can only say that although the techniques of modern civil procedure may be in harmony with the culture of a free people, criminal procedure, even in the states that claim to be democratic, has not yet progressed beyond the practices of absolutism, or one might even say beyond the brutal instincts of the barbarian horde.

The cruel absurdity of the death penalty, demonstrated in the middle of the eighteenth century by an Italian,[10] has been abolished only in Italy and in a few other states faithful to Cesare Beccaria; but the great powers that dominate the world still employ it, while paying lip service to the theory that the basis of their political organization is the equal moral dignity of all men and the inviolability of the human personality.

In criminal procedure as we see it applied, the accused is still an inert object at the mercy of the inquisitor's violence. The death penalty, which makes possible the irremediable murder of an innocent man, is a legalized crime. Even when it does not lead to the imposition of the death penalty, however, criminal pro-

[10] Cesare Beccaria, *Dei delitti e delle pene,* republished with preface and notes by Piero Calamandrei (Firenze: Le Monnier, 1945).

cedure is nothing but a series of brutal incursions within the supposedly inviolate sphere of the human personality. Physical coercion is still the preferred method of the inquisitor. Held incommunicado during the period of questioning, the accused is alone with his examiners, without aid of counsel; torture, although formally abolished, has returned under new guises more scientific but nonetheless cruel: the third degree, endless hours of incessant questioning, truth serum. And in the majority of prisons the world over the punishments are still brutally afflictive and inhuman.

There is a long road ahead before the reforms called for in our constitution can be put into effect, before "any physical or moral violence against persons whose liberty is restricted is prohibited" (Art. 13) or before penal provisions contrary to "the sentiments of humanity" are no longer permitted (Art. 27).

In the civil procedure of the most progressive nations, every man, even when appearing before the judge, is treated as a person. In the criminal procedure, whether he is before the inquisitor who interrogates him, the jailer who imprisons him, or the executioner who takes his life, man is still only a thing.

"There is no liberty whenever the laws permit that under certain conditions man ceases to be a person and becomes a thing."[11] I never tire of repeating this sentence of Cesare Beccaria at every opportunity, because it seems to me that in these apparently simple words there lies the hope of mankind and the program of the future.

In concluding this short study of the judicial process, I should like to make a general remark that is not only valid for this process but can be a fitting goal for all fields of human activity:

Each of us must act to the best of his ability in his own field so that men of all classes and all countries cease to be things

[11] *Ibid.*, Sec. XXVII.

and become persons; each must strive so that from every man there may radiate a sentiment of understanding and sympathy that enables the inhabitants of every continent to recognize one another as brothers.